KIDDING AROUND

SPAIN

A YOUNG PERSON'S GUIDE

BETSEY BIGGS

ILLUSTRATED BY ANTHONY D'AGOSTINO

John Muir Publications
Santa Fe, New Mexico

For my family—for everything—and for Big Al, who told me I could do it.

Thanks to all amoeba everywhere, especially Jason and Eduardo, and to the folks at Dial. And special thanks to all the kids at the American School of Madrid and in the Guadix barrio.

John Muir Publications, P.O. Box 613, Santa Fe, NM 87504

First edition. First printing.

Library of Congress Cataloging-in-Publication Data
Biggs, Betsey.
    Kidding around Spain   :   a young person's guide to the country / Betsey Biggs;   illustrated by Anthony D'Agostino.
        p.   cm.
    Summary: Describes the history and cultural background of Spain, as well as the sights young people would find particularly interesting.
        ISBN 0-945465-97-1
    1. Spain—Description and travel—1981-   —Guidebooks—Juvenile literature. [1. Spain—Description and travel—Guides.] I. D'Agostino, Anthony (Anthony R.), ill. II. Title.
DP43.B52   1991
914.604'83—dc20   91-16770
                                                                         CIP
                                                                          AC

Designer: Joanna V. Hill
Typeface: Trump Medieval
Typesetter: Copygraphics, Inc., Santa Fe, New Mexico
Printer: Guynes Printing Company of New Mexico

Distributed to the book trade by
W.W. Norton & Company, Inc.
New York, New York

Contents

1. Land of Many Rabbits

¡**Habla Español!** *Language is a tricky thing in Spain. There are four languages spoken here: Castellano (also known as Español), Catalán, Basque, and Gallego. In fact, for many Spanish people, Castellano is a second language. Of course, almost everyone speaks it fluently.*

When the first Mediterranean voyagers got to Spain and Portugal, they called it "Iberia," meaning Land of Water (they came from the desert). Their coins featured the plentiful rabbit, but it wasn't until the Carthaginians came that the land was named Hispania, Land of Many Rabbits. As language evolved, it became known as España. Today's Spain is a blend of old and new, of Africa and Europe, of tradition and change. You'll find castles that have been standing for hundreds, or possibly thousands, of years. There are even cave paintings that have been estimated to be 25,000 years old! You'll also run into skyscrapers, movie theaters, and fast food.

Until 1469, when King Ferdinand and Queen Isabella got married and unified Spain (and when Columbus encountered America a few years later), no one had really thought about its kingdoms forming a nation. Some provinces are still fighting for their independence. Look for different customs in the places you visit. You'll soon see that there's more than one Spain.

If this is the first time you've been to a different country, you'll be confused when you hear

people chatting away in a language that you don't understand. This can be weird, but have no fear. It's not hard to communicate, as long as you know a few basic phrases. Some people you meet will probably speak some English, but others won't know a word. Anyone will appreciate your trying out their language—and it's fun, too! There are Spanish phrases in the back of this book to help you get started. When all else fails, make-up-your-own sign language can be a life-saver and a lesson in communication.

One of the best things about being in a foreign country is noticing what you all have in common. Do you see kids playing soccer after school? What about the grocery store or the musicians on the street? You may find just as many similarities between you and your Spanish friends as you do differences! A good thing to do while you're traveling is to keep a journal of your trip. Use any notebook, or find a scrapbook that you can put snapshots into later. Drawings can be even better than photos—use your imagination.

Spain's got everything: beaches to splash through, snowy mountains to climb, and cities that hum with both history and modern life. As a matter of fact, there's so much here that no one could do or see it all in a lifetime. This book shows you some of the places you're likely to visit and helps you discover all there is to see and do there. But don't forget that one of the joys of traveling is doing your own exploring. Some of the neatest places in Spain are little villages set by the mountains or on a ridge, in the middle of nowhere. So if you find yourself in a place not explored in this book, congratulations. Have fun making your own discoveries!

Rowdy Royal! King Juan Carlos is a down-to-earth kind of guy. For example, he used to ride his motor-cycle around Madrid late at night (his bodyguards hated it). And when he skis at Baqueira/Beret, he waits in line, just like everybody else. Look out!

2. A Step Back in Time

Prehistoric tribes were hunters and gatherers. They used charcoal and animal grease to paint bisons, horses, fish, and other symbols on cave walls at Altamira, Puente Viesgo, and Cueva de la Pileta.

3000-300 B.C.—North Africans, Phoenicians, Celts, Greeks, and Carthaginians colonize what is now Spain and Portugal, bringing new blood and the names "Iberia" and "Hispania" to the peninsula.

209 B.C.—Romans take over "Ispania," dropping the H. They bring Roman law, wine, and language and build bridges, aqueducts, and roads. Cities such as Toledum (Toledo) and Tarragona are founded. Christians and Jews arrive, and in 325, when the Roman emperor converts to Christianity, so does Roman Spain.

A.D. 409—Vandals from the North brutally ravage Roman Spain, inventing the word "Vandalism." Soon after, other northerners called Visigoths overtake the Vandals and establish a slightly calmer dynasty, trying to achieve the Romans' status. But no dice for the barbarians.

711—Newly converted Moslem Moors invade Ispania through the Straits of Gibraltar and kill Visigothic King Roderick in battle. Within ten years, they have conquered almost the entire peninsula.

718—The Christians turn back the Moors at Covadonga and establish the Kingdom of Asturias, in the Cantabrian mountains.

785-1002—Moorish Córdoba is the largest, wealthiest city in Europe. The Moors live with Jews and Christians in tolerance. La Mezquita mosque is built here from ruined columns around the world. Royalty and the rich come from all over Europe for Córdoba's up-to-date hospitals. Meanwhile, the Asturian Christians spread south, establishing two new kingdoms, León and Castile.

1085—King Alfonso VI defeats the Moors at Toledo. The Moorish Almoravides come to the rescue but are intolerant of the Jews and Christians living under Moorish rule.

1094-1099—El Cid takes Valencia from the Moors and rules until his death.

1130—Alfonso VII establishes a multicultural school in Toledo so that Moorish, Jewish, and Christian scholars can exchange ideas.

1146—The Almohades invade from Morocco and take over Moorish Sevilla. They turn it into an incredible city and learning center, but their intolerence drives many Jews and Christians to Christian Spain.

1188—León establishes the first Spanish Corte (representational congress).

1212—King Alfonso VIII of Castile defeats the Moors at Navas de Tolosa in southeast Spain. Everyone realizes that it's the beginning of the end for the Moors.

1243—University of Salamanca opens its doors.

1348—The Black Death (an epidemic otherwise known as the Plague) hits, killing about one-third of Spain's people.

1469—Queen Isabella of Castile marries King Ferdinand of Aragon, uniting most of Spain under one flag. They are called *Los Reyes Católicos*—the Catholic Monarchs.

1480—The Spanish Inquisition begins. Moorish and Jewish converts are tortured and killed if it's suspected that they don't believe in Christ. Even a hot bath is enough to get you thrown in jail.

1492—Columbus discovers America. Jews are expelled from Spain. And Ferdinand and Isabella capture Granada, the Moors' last city, after a ten-year battle.

1502—Moslems still in Spain are told to get out or convert to Christianity. Most convert and are then called *moriscos*.

1519—In the New World, Cortés defeats the Aztec Indians and creates New Spain, or Mexico. A few years later, Pizarro conquers the Inca Indians in Peru. Mines in both colonies send silver and gold back to Spain.

1561—King Philip II moves the capital of Spain to Madrid. He builds El Escorial as a royal burial tomb.

1588—The Spanish Armada sails to England and is soundly defeated by the British.

1605—Cervantes publishes the world's first novel, *Don Quixote*.

1609—Moriscos are forced to leave Spain.

1700—The French Bourbon dynasty takes over the Spanish throne.

1704—Britain takes the Rock of Gibraltar.

1808—The French invade Spain, and Napoleon puts his brother Joseph (José) on the Spanish throne. Goya does his *Disasters of War* paintings.

1810—New World colonies begin to assert their independence. By 1826, they are all free of Spain.

1812—Spain's first constitution is written by the Cortes (parliament).

1820—The Spanish Inquisition is abolished. The army decrees constitutional government. King Ferdinand VII leaves but regains the throne in 1823.

1873-1874—Spain's First Republic fails miserably, and the people demand a king. King Alfonso XII takes over.

1923-1930—General Primo de Rivera overthrows the government and rules with an iron hand.

1931—Spain's Second Republic is declared after elections show that nobody wants kings or dictators anymore. King Alfonso XIII flees the country. The government has high hopes but tries to change things too fast. Left-wing atheists and right-wing saboteurs burn churches and attack landowners. The country starts separating into two factions: Republican and Nationalist.

1936-1939—The Spanish Civil War. General Francisco Franco leads a Moroccan army to attack Republican forces. After three bloody years and almost a million lost lives, the Republicans surrender to Franco's Nationalist force. Picasso's mural, *Guernica*, depicts the horror of the war but has to be sent to the U.S. so it doesn't get destroyed.

1939-1975—The Franco dictatorship. Independence movements are stifled and General Franco rules with an iron fist. Unbelievably, he dies of old age.

1975—King Juan Carlos I comes to power at Franco's death. He slowly establishes democracy.

1977—First postwar elections are held. Moderates win big.

1981—Army officers attempt a coup, but the king thwarts them.

1982—Second elections are held. Socialist Felipe Gonzalez is elected prime minister by a huge majority. Madrid hosts soccer's World Cup.

1984—Spain joins NATO (OTAN, in Spanish).

1988—Spain joins the European Community (EC). Barcelona plans for the Olympics and Sevilla plans for Expo 92, celebrating the 500th anniversary of Columbus's voyage.

1992—The 1992 Summer Olympics in Barcelona. Expo 92 Universal Fair in Sevilla. Madrid is the cultural capital of Europe.

3. Taking the Bull by the Horns in Madrid

Madrid's Metro system (subway) is fast, clean, and cheap, especially if you buy a ten-ride pass. It will take you wherever you want to go. At night, you may want to hop in a cab. If so, watch for the green "Libre" sign.

hy is Madrid the capital of Spain? It's freezing here in the winter and burning in the summer. There are no coasts and no rivers (to speak of). Give up? Because it's right smack in the middle of Spain, a symbol of the country's unification. At least that's what King Philip II thought when he moved the court here in 1561. During the Franco years, Madrid was the official center of power. But then, since Barcelona was closer to France and farther from the terrible Franco dictatorship, it became the cultural center of Spain, leaving Madrid as a large, ugly backwater. In the past twenty years, however, Madrid has turned itself into one of Europe's great cities—full of culture, good food, and plenty of street life.

From Zero to Twenty-Six in No Time Flat
The **Puerto del Sol**—a Spanish Times Square— is right smack in the center of Madrid, and of Spain, too. Zero in on the Kilometer Zero plaque in front of the Communidad de Madrid building. All Spanish highways start here: this is the *exact* center of Spain. On the other side of the traffic jam you'll discover a friendlier emblem, a sculp-

*On **New Year's Eve** (*Nochevieja), the Puerto del Sol is closed to traffic and filled with Madrileños of every size, shape, and color cheering the New Year on. At each stroke of midnight they have to eat a grape (*uva). *Twelve in a row! Easier said than done.*

Near Plaza Mayor is Cava de San Miguel, *a street with lots of signs saying **"Mesón de..."** These fun tapas bars have live Spanish music and yummy snacks to eat with toothpicks. But don't come for breakfast or lunch, because they don't even open until about nine at night.*

ture called "The Bear and the Bush." Madrid's biggest department store, **El Corte Inglés**, is right next door. Local kids say the record store is great. Hang out and see what's hot.

Hungry? The Puerto del Sol is littered with fast food joints, but it's more fun to order a sandwich at the **Museo de Jamón** (Ham Museum) on Calle San Jerónimo. Over 100 varieties of ham hang from the ceiling at this speedy lunch spot. They also have great vegetarian sandwiches! Wander down nearby Calle Victoria if you're on the lookout for bullfight tickets or atmosphere.

You'll pass plenty of souvenir shops on your way down Calle Mayor. Look to your left for the arches that lead into Madrid's famous **Plaza Mayor**. This 400-year-old square has seen plenty of history in its time, from bullfights to Inquisition executions. The balconies above were the VIP seats. These days, the main activity seems to be visiting the tourist office—Turismo—or people-watching from cafés.

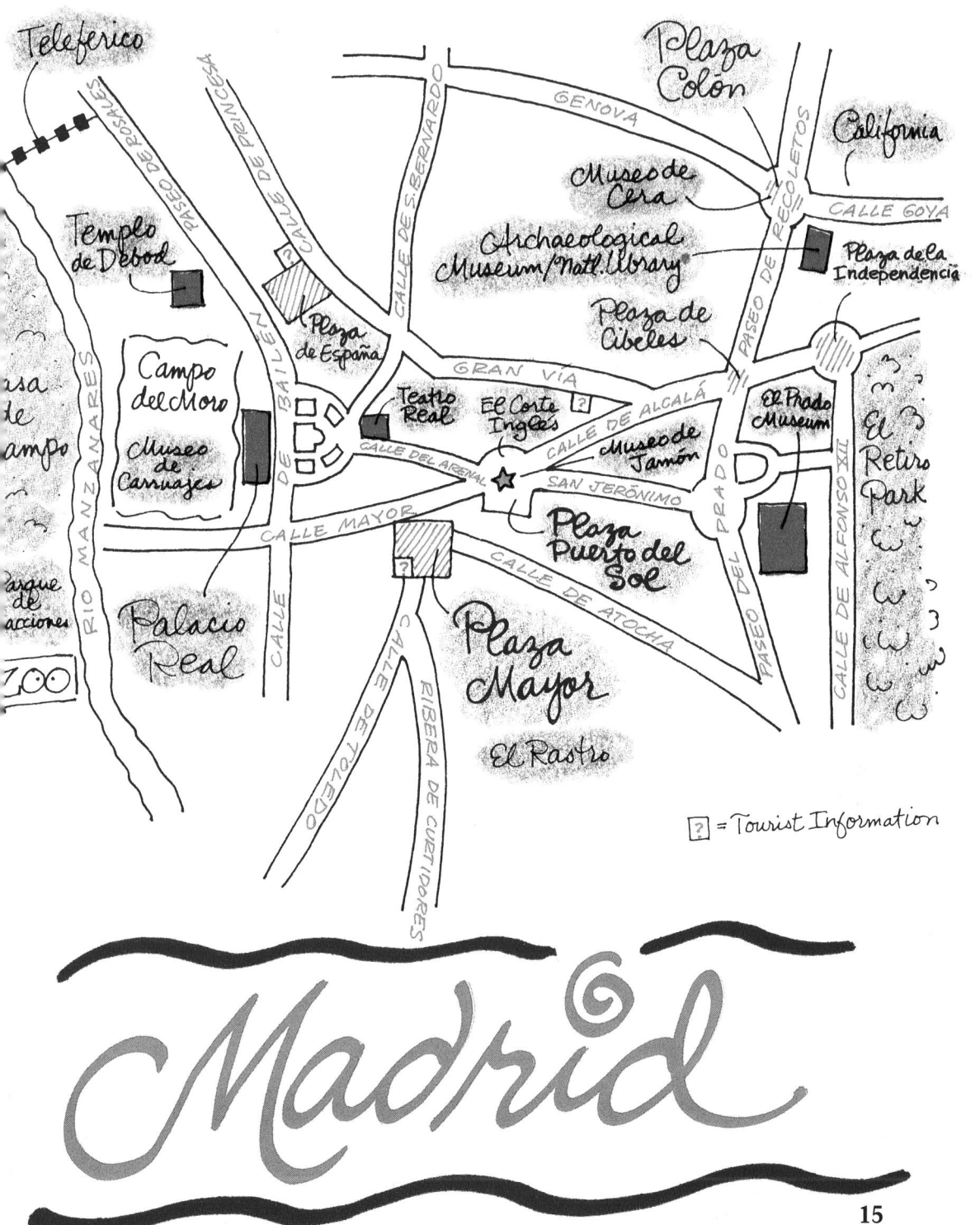

15

*Sunday is fun day in Madrid. The Plaza Mayor is home to Europe's biggest and best **stamp and coin market**. Sometimes they sell cheap stuff as well as rarities, but even if you don't buy anything, it's fun to watch. And if you're after clothes, souvenirs, antiques, and other assorted junk, just wander the streets of the **Rastro**, Europe's largest flea market.*

Walk down the Arco de Cuchilleros to the world's oldest restaurant, **Casa Botín**. They've been serving dinner here every night since 1725. That's a lot of food! Look for their certificate from the Guinness Book of World Records, and don't miss the ancient wood-fire oven where everything is cooked. Botín's was a favorite of writer Ernest Hemingway. If you're not much into roast suckling pig or spending wads of cash on dinner, then go next door to **El Cuchi**. You'll recognize it by the "Hemingway Never Ate Here" sign on the door.

Near the end of Calle Mayor, the **Palacio Real** rises in the distance. If you're lucky, they'll be changing the guard (this happens twice a week). No one's actually lived here since 1931, but the palace is still used for state occasions, like the signing of Spain's entry into the European Community. It's fun to see the fancy **Sala de Trono** (throne room) and Royal Clock Collection, but don't leave yet! The **Armería**'s frozen war boasts over a hundred full suits of armor, including horse, kid, and dog armor. And the **Farmacia** has some of Europe's oldest potions and perfumes.

Work those sightseeing bugs out of your system at **Campo del Moro Park**, behind the palace. Besides the green grass and fresh air, you'll also find the **Museo de Carruajes**, which has royal horse-drawn carriages dating back to the 1500s.

The **Plaza de España** is famous for its two skyscrapers, the Torre de Madrid and the Edificio España. Enjoy the view and a snack at the **Edificio España's 26th floor café**. Below you'll see a statue of Spanish author Cervantes with his two most famous characters, Don Quixote and Sancho Panza. And tons of microscopic people.

16

The Broadway of Madrid

Gran Vía is a wide and noisy street that starts at the Plaza de España. Between the neon and the traffic, you'll see huge movie billboards that are still painted by hand. See if you can recognize any recent movies by their Spanish titles. One of the world's fanciest **McDonald's** is at the corner of Calle Montera and Gran Vía. Ascend the sprawling marble staircase with elegance, grace, and a Big Mac.

The Gran Vía ends at the **Plaza de Cibeles**, not far from the Prado and other museums. If your feet are exhausted and your throat parched, you've come to the right place. The **Círculo de Bellas Artes Café** has tall, cool drinks and comfy leather couches to sprawl out on. You'll pay to get in, but it's worth it, especially if you want to see any of its many art exhibits.

Paintings, Paseos, and the Park

El Prado is one of the world's biggest art museums—over 5,000 paintings! You'd better not try to see everything at once (drive this point home with your grown-up ahead of time). It's better to spread your visit out over a couple of days. Before you do anything, get a good museum map at the entrance and check out the postcards at the gift shop to see which paintings you'd like to see. The ground floor is home to medieval Spanish art. Look for *retablos*, ancient comic strips that taught illiterate peasants the stories of the Bible. The storyline is sometimes easy to guess, and you'll definitely recognize the gory demons from the late late show.

Upstairs, head for the paintings by **Hieronymous Bosch** (the Spaniards call him "El Bosco").

*The **Real Fábrica de Tapices** has been hand-making tapestries in the same way since the 1700s. Visiting this factory is a fun way to see just how tapestries are woven. It takes three or four months for one person to weave just one square meter, with thousands of colors to keep track of. No wonder prices start at $60,000.*

A meadow‽ El Prado means "The Meadow" in Spanish. The area around here was once a beautiful meadow. Today, zooming traffic has replaced chirping birds!

Temple of Doom! *The Egyptian **Temple of Debod** in Parque del Oeste (West Park) was a gift from the Egyptian government to Spain in thanks for some help from Spanish archaeologists. It was shipped from Egypt stone by stone and carefully rebuilt. Now it's one of Madrid's oldest buildings! Peek inside to see the spooky Egyptian inscriptions and tombs.*

You'll have fun picking out all the weird details in these colorful paintings. Look for the "bird feeder," the pig dressed as a nun, and other wacky details in *The Garden of Earthly Delights*.

Famous Spanish artist **Diego de Velázquez** was King Philip IV's court painter. He painted realistic portraits of dwarfs, royal kids, and other court life. Look for his painting of the young prince on horseback.

A later court painter, **Francisco Goya**, had a different style. Since he disliked his patrons, King Carlos V and Queen Maria Luisa, he painted ugly portraits of them. He also painted colorful pictures called "cartoons" that were turned into tapestries. But Goya's most gruesome paintings are the "black paintings" he did right before he died. Rumor has it that *Saturn Devouring His Son* hung above his dining room table. Yuck!

The **Paseo del Prado** may be named for the monster art museum, but the Prado is not the only museum on the street. Between the trees and fountains you'll find others: the **Museo Postal** (behind the wedding-cake Post Office), **Museo Naval** (next door), the **Museo del Ejército** (army museum), and the **Museo Nacional de Artes Decorativas** (just off the Paseo). In the middle of the street are the fountains of Cibeles, Apollo, and Neptuno, all Roman gods.

Whew! All that sightseeing can be a drain. Energize at **Chocolates Godiva** in the Galeria del Prado mall and then head for the giant green space of **El Retiro Park**. This is the perfect place to toss a frisbee, eat a sandwich, or just goof off. Toss the ducks your crusts, or quack 'em up with your rowing skills.

Lights, Camera, Action!
Want to keep up with the latest movies? V.O., or Original Version, means a movie hasn't been dubbed into Spanish. Most of Madrid's V.O. movies are shown near the Plaza de España. To get into the spirit of things, you could stop at **Foster's Hollywood** *for a Bacon Double Cheeseburger or Super-Duper Star-Spangled Banana Split, starring their yummy hot fudge. There are other Hollywood restaurants in Madrid and throughout Spain.*

Pablo Picasso painted **Guernica** *during the Spanish Civil War after the Nazis helped Franco and the Nationalists bomb the entire Basque town of Guernica. The painting was outlawed by Franco and was displayed in the Museum of Modern Art in New York until 1984, when it returned to Madrid. You'll find it in the Casón del Buen Retiro, an annex of the Prado across the street from the big museum. It's still so controversial that it's kept behind bullet-proof glass. Look carefully at Picasso's images of frightened people, horses, and cattle and think about how war can affect ordinary people.*

Uptown Action

North of the park is one of Madrid's ritziest neighborhoods, the barrio of **Salamanca**. Jet-set shoppers share the streets with bankers and diplomatic types. Go to **California** on Calle Goya for good breakfasts and snacks upstairs and a bookstore downstairs. Its red volcanic ceiling and high-tech furniture make it look like the set for a remake of the Jetsons, but the Jetsons never had free video games!

Paseo de Recoletos is really the same street as Paseo del Prado. To its east, there's a gigantic building separated into two halves. The side facing Paseo de Recoletos is the National Library, which is not only boring but unvisitable. The other side, facing Calle Serrano, is Madrid's fantabulous **Museo Arqueológico Nacional**. With everything from ancient Egyptian mummies to Roman mosaics and medieval Spanish art, you can walk through time. End your visit with a

trip to the famous **Altamira cave paintings**—or at least a good fake. The actual 25,000-year-old cave paintings located in Cantabria are now closed to the public because humidity from everybody's breath was causing damage. So archaeologists have re-created both the paintings and the cave to give you a good chance to see Planet Earth's first artists. Lean back and enjoy the show.

Plaza Colón is home to the **Jardínes del Descubrimiento**. Huge stone tablets show pieces of New World diaries, and below the plaza you'll find a cool "Columbus cave" with a loud rushing waterfall and a 3-D map of the explorer's travels. Back on top you'll see plenty of Madrileños walking, shopping, eating, drinking, and skateboarding.

Across the street is the **Museo de Cera**. This wax museum is a great place to catch up on your Spanish history, especially if you buy the museum

*If you're the sci-fi type, you'll want to head to Madrid's **Natural Science Museum**. This place is stuffed with fun computer programs, giant dinosaur bones, and glow-in-the-dark rocks. If astronomy makes you starry-eyed, go to the **Planetarium**, farther away. You'll probably agree that it's worth it as you seemingly zoom into outer space with an alien spaceship.*

Los Toros, *or bullfights,*
are popular in Spain, espe-
cially in Castilla and
Andalucía. While bull-
fighting is commonly
called a sport, it's really a
ritual. No matter what
happens, the bull will
definitely be slaughtered.
Many people think bull-
fights are stupid and
cruel, while others find
them exciting. There's no
doubt that they're an
important part of Spanish
culture. If you do go, don't
sit too close—especially
if you're an animal lover.

guidebook for a few hundred pesetas. Wander through halls full of Spanish royalty, murderers, New World conquistadors, and modern types like astronaut Neil Armstrong and Snoopy.

Matadors, Goalies, and Corn-on-the-Cob
Las Ventas is Spain's biggest bullfight ring. Bull-fights happen every Sunday, April to October, and during special fiestas. If you come early, check out the bullfighting history museum. You'll find bulls' heads, matadors' capes, and other gory toro stuff. If you'd rather cheer for soccer players than toro killers, then you'll want to head for **Estadio Santiago Bernabeu**. Soccer (called *fútbol* here) is Spain's most popular sport and Real Madrid is the hometown team. After the game, polish off BBQ ribs, corn-on-the-cob, and grandma's apple pie to country western tunes at **Alfredo's Barbacoa**. Alfredo is a down-home American who's lived in Spain for over twenty years. If you can't stand another menu full of oxtails and eels, this one will make you cheer.

22

This Is a City Park?

Hop onto the metro or the Paseo de Rosales teleférico (cable car) headed for **Casa de Campo Park**. Before you know it, you'll have left the big city behind. Casa de Campo is over ten times bigger than El Retiro—4,300 acres, to be exact.

The **Zoo de Madrid** has everything from dolphin shows to lumbering giant pandas. You can take it in by boat, mini-train, dromedary, or good old foot. If you do see a dolphin show, stick around downstairs for a backstage look at the performers. There's dolphin info in both Spanish and English.

Ciudad de Niños (Kid's City) is a fantastic hands-on museum designed just for kids. It's next to the lake, called **El Lago** in Castellano. Stretch out your arms on the Lago rowboats or your legs on the paths around it. And when you're done with fresh air, try out the **Parque de Attracciones** for size. Just follow the roller coaster screams.

*Gloom Tomb. El Escorial is a giant monastery not far from Madrid. Local kids say it's dark, gloomy, and boring, but remember, it's this way because it was King Philip II's Spanish Inquisition headquarters. The **Valley of the Fallen**, near El Escorial, is supposed to be a memorial to the Civil War victims on both sides. But the fact that it's where dictator General Franco is buried makes it unpopular with some folks.*

4. Around Madrid: Spanish Castle Magic

Draw a circle around Madrid and you'll find some of Spain's best cities inside it. They may be in different provinces, but the feel is the same. You have reached the heartland. This was Spain's battlefield for hundreds of years: the Christians kept pushing the Moors south and populating the country. The castles you'll see scattered around are reminders that they had to guard their new territory *very* carefully.

The Rhyme That Lied.
You may have heard "the rain in Spain falls mainly on the plain." It's a good tongue exercise, but it just isn't true. The Castilian plain (or meseta*) is actually dry and rugged.*

Aranjuez
Aranjuez is not only an oasis from the Madrid summers but the strawberry capital of Spain. Though it's fun to explore the **Palacio Real** and **Casa del Labrador** (which is *hardly* a farmhouse), the best parts of Aranjuez are its river and endless parks. In fact, the lawn in front of the Casa del Labrador begs to be rolled upon. Drift into the **Casa Marina** to find out what a royal rowboat looks like and brave a creaking, rocking storm room. If you feel your sea legs calling you, cross the rickety footbridge to the paddleboats that are available for rent.

Whatever you do at Aranjuez, *don't* miss the strawberry stands. Ask for *freson con nata* (cream) or *helados* (ice cream). Mmm mmm good.

All of the towns in this chapter are within a few hours of Madrid and can be visited as day trips, as well as overnight. If you're day tripping from Madrid, find out about **RENFE's Tren Turistica** (Tourist Train) packages.

You get a round-trip train ticket, entry fees paid, and a tour. The trips are best for hard-to-get-to spots like Cuenca's Ciudad Encantada and the Monasterio de Piedra. But train-lovers will get all steamed up about the

Strawberry Train, an antique wooden steam train that visits the strawberry capital of Spain, Aranjuez. Local kids say it's a "berry" fun trip.

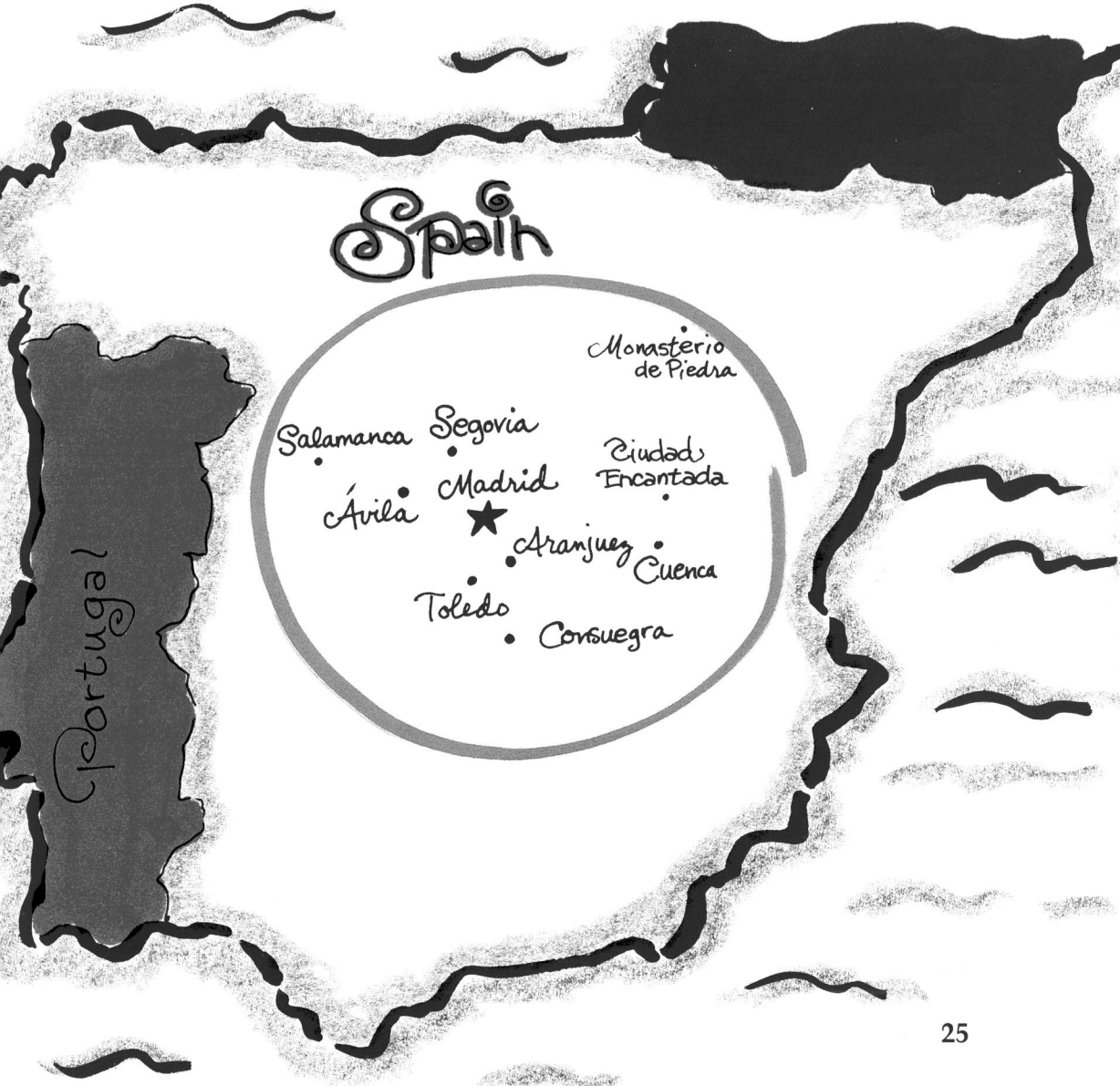

Toledo (not the one in Ohio) is a great place to get lost. In the Middle Ages, it was the home of Spanish royalty, and any house you see probably has its share of stories.

Toledo's most famous resident was El Greco ("The Greek"), a Greek painter who lived in Toledo from 1577 to 1614. You'll see his paintings hung all over town. El Greco's most famous painting is *The Burial of the Count of Orgaz*. It sits in an annex of the nearby **Church of Santo Tomé**. Look for his self-portrait (the only guy staring at the "camera") and his son's portrait (the only kid). The **Casa del Greco** isn't really his house, but it's still interesting to see how people lived 400 years ago. Compare a new city map to El Greco's map, and you'll see that Toledo hasn't changed much in all that time.

Toledo's **Cathedral** was Castile's royal church for hundreds of years. Try to count the pillars holding up the building. If you come at the right time, you'll catch the sun lighting up fluffy angels and clouds through the hole of the *transparente* behind the altar.

Toledo was famous for its tricultural mix: Moorish, Jewish, and Christian. Wander around the *judería*, or Jewish section. The **Sephardic Museum** is a good place to find out more about Spanish Jews. It's built inside a beautiful synagogue called El Tránsito. Many of Toledo's houses were also built by Moors under Christian rule.

Walking around, you'll quickly see that Toledo lives up to its reputation as the souvenir capital of Spain. Swords, suits of armor, and sweet marzipan candy line the streets. If you want to take something home, look around to make sure

A tasty view of Toledo can be found along the Carretera de Circunvalación. Sit on the terrace at the parador and have a sunset snack.

Look out above! See those funny-looking red hats hanging from the ceiling all over Toledo cathedral? There's a spooky explanation: when Spanish cardinals died, they were allowed to be buried anywhere they chose and their hats placed above their grave forever, until they rotted away. So that's why they're rotting—and that's what you're standing on!

you're getting a good price. The best places are usually the workshops where you can watch a sword get hammered into shape or see craftsmen make a piece of furniture. There's no charge just to watch.

La Mancha

The plains of La Mancha seem to stretch out forever, broken up only by broken-down windmills, castles, and tractors. Spain's most famous book, *Don Quixote*, was set here. The hero rides through the dust with his faithful servant, trying to knock down the windmills he thinks are giants. **Consuegra** is the perfect place to appreciate La Mancha. Head to the top of town to discover the silent castle and windmills (*molinos*). Poke around, and notice what *doesn't* lie beyond the town borders.

Ávila and Salamanca

Climb to the top of Ávila's walls and you'll feel as tall as a giant spying on the people below and the lizards on top. To see how anyone was ever able to build over a mile of forty-foot wall before bulldozers were invented, visit the **Museo Provincial** in the Casa de los Deanes. You'll discover how the blocks were cracked and cut from early quarries. You'll also see exhibits of everything from medieval costumes to ancient Iberian gravestones shaped like pigs.

Ávila's most famous resident was Saint Teresa, who turned the Catholic church on its ear in the sixteenth century. In the **Convento de Santa Teresa**, which you can get to by the scenic Rastro walk, they've preserved some of her belongings, including one of her fingers, a creepy, bony rem-

Bloody graffiti! *If you're wondering what the red graffiti on the university walls in Salamanca is all about, be prepared for a grisly answer. For centuries, graduating Ph.D.'s have celebrated by killing and roasting a bull for a huge feast and writing their names and titles on the town walls in bulls' blood. It's now forbidden, but old habits die hard. Yuck.*

nant. Speaking of gross, Ávila's traditional candy, *yemas*, consists of mushy, candied egg yolks. Feeling brave?

Ávila is about halfway between Madrid and Salamanca. Until the 1700s, the Universidad de Salamanca was considered one of the top three universities in Europe (i.e., the world, at least according to Europeans). Today, you'll find lots of American students studying (or just hanging out) in this college town. The **Patio de las Escuelas** gate to the university is decorated with flowers, twirls, and a hidden frog that brings good luck to test-takers.

Next door to the university's no-nonsense classrooms is the **Escuela Menor**, or high school. There's a beautiful cloister (or courtyard) here, but don't miss the zodiac ceiling in the small **Museo del Universidad**, inside. This beautiful painting depicts the stars from Aquarius to Taurus. What's your sign?

Salamanca doesn't have a **cathedral**—it's got two! The new cathedral is fancier outside, but the old one (connected) is more beautiful inside. What do you think?

If you'd rather see freshmen than frescoes, turn toward **Plaza Mayor**. People say that this is the best people-watching plaza in all of Spain. It's constantly filled with artists, students, and musicians. In fact, it's so crowded it's hard to believe that until 1863 they held bullfights here.

Segovia

Look at a map and you'll see that Segovia is shaped like a ship. The stern is the **Roman Aqueduct**, which carried water to the city for almost 2,000 years. No one knows how the Romans were able to build it without a drop of mortar or cement. Walking up Calle de Cervantes, you'll see the tall mast of the **Cathedral** ahead of you. But it's the figurehead of the ship—the **Alcázar**—that steals the show. It's just what you always thought a castle should look like, with knights in shining armor and towers armed with waving flags. Have fun exploring.

If you ever wanted to be one of the Knights of the Round Table, take a hike from the Alcázar to the 12-sided **Vera Cruz Church**. You can see it from the castle towers. The Knights Templar founded the church in the 1200s. As part of their initiation, every knight had to watch over a supposed piece of the true cross through the night. Climb up to the tower for a noble view of the castle and city beyond.

Cuenca and Ciudad Encantada

The cliff-hanging houses of Cuenca are strung precariously over the Huecar River. You can visit one of these *casas colgadas* by going into the **Museo de Arte Abstracto Español**. But there's more here than just the view. Optical illusions and a glow-in-the-dark room could change your mind about modern art.

After you've tested the footbridge, head north to Ciudad Encantada (Enchanted City). Rain, ice, snow, and wind have all helped to erode these rocks into some very strange shapes, as you can tell by their names—*El Perro* (The Dog) and *Mar de Piedra* (Sea of Stone). This Star Trek setting lets both your legs and your imagination run wild.

*You won't believe your eyes or ears when you arrive at the **Monasterio de Piedra** after a dusty drive. The monks who lived here devoted their lives to creating a watery oasis from just one stream. They built canals, waterfalls, and grottoes that you can see today. Other parts of the park are great for picnicking or zoning out to the sound of gurgling water. When you've quenched your thirst for green, visit the remains of the Stone Monastery and its tower. Would-be monks can even stay in part of the monastery, now that it's a hotel.*

5. Northern Spain: Bagpipes and Beaches, Basques and Bikes

S pain's north coast stretches from the Pyrenees and the proud Basque country through the beaches of Cantabria and the snowy Asturian mountains to the fishing villages of Galicia. You'll find everything from beaches to ski resorts on your way to the end of the world. But the North is big country, so don't be afraid to do your own exploring (with a grown-up, of course).

Galicia

Galicia, on Spain's west coast, is not what you'd expect Spain to look like. Its green hills and fishing villages remind most people of Ireland. And the language, Gallego, is closer to Portuguese than to Spanish. Long peninsulas have created the warm Gallego *rías* that line the sea. These mini-seas are great for smooth swimming.

A Coruña may be Galicia's main city and Pontevedra its capital, but **Santiago de Compostela** is the heartbeat of Galicia. Hang around the **cathedral** for a while, and you'll probably see some modern pilgrims paying their respects to Santiago. Put your hand on the **Tree of Jesse** where millions of hands have worn down five smooth holes, and think about all the people who have been in this spot before you. The

*Getaway. . . If you're in Galicia in May or June, try and see the **curros** that take place in the villages between Bayona and La Guardia. These fiestas feature local men riding through swarms of wild horses at dawn, rounding them up, branding them, and setting them free again. The people of the villages celebrate with huge feasts and music. Ask at Turismo for dates and details.*

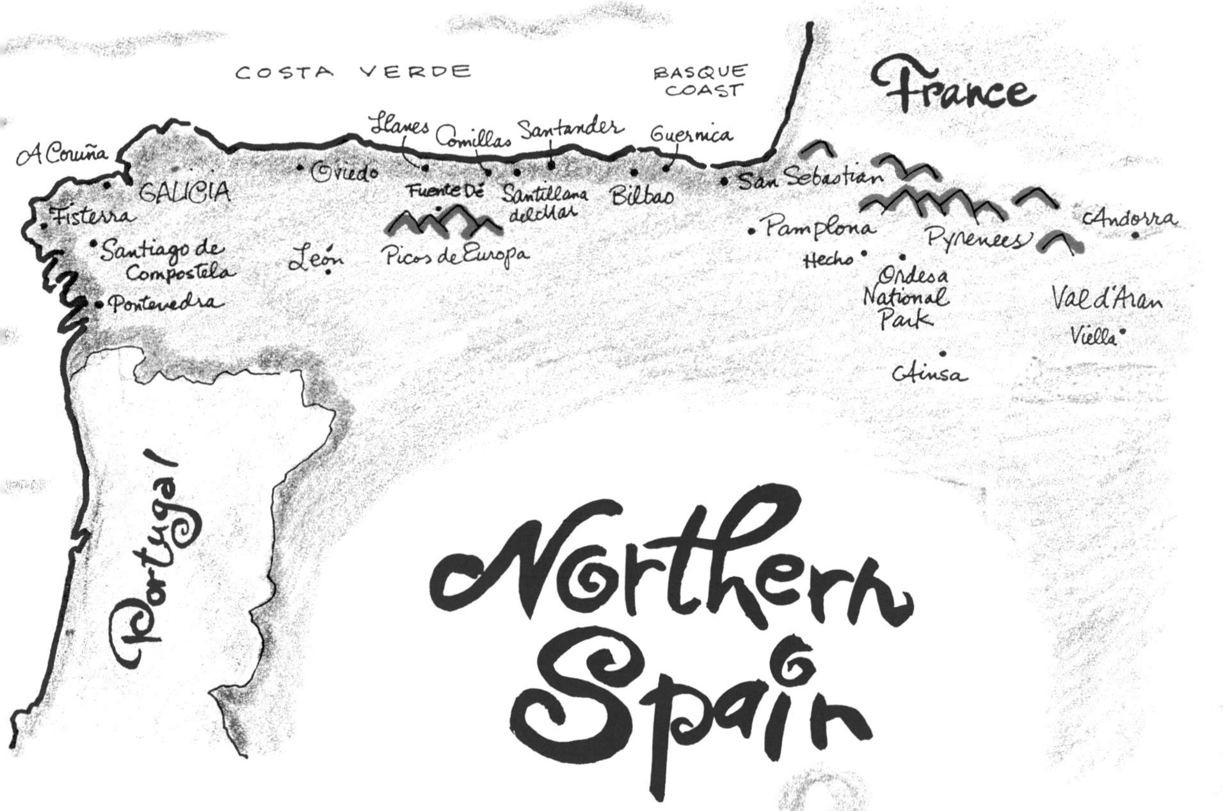

Northern Spain

COSTA VERDE — BASQUE COAST — France

A Coruña · Fisterra · GALICIA · Santiago de Compostela · Pontevedra · León · Oviedo · Llanes · Comillas · Santander · Guernica · San Sebastián · Fuente Dé · Santillana del Mar · Bilbao · Picos de Europa · Pamplona · Hecho · Ordesa National Park · Ainsa · Pyrenees · Andorra · Val d'Aran · Viella · Portugal

statue of the original architect, Maestro Mateo, crouches on the other side of the Tree of Jesse. Pilgrims kiss his head for wisdom. Also check out the cathedral's huge rope pulley system, which is needed to pull the huge *Botafumeiro* incense burner through the cathedral. Long ago they used incense to fight the smell of hundreds of pilgrims who hadn't showered for months or even years (early Christians thought that bathing was evil). But today the system is only used on special occasions. The rest of the time it sits in the museum.

If you wander the mossy streets of the old section long enough, it's easy to forget about the modern world. Look for *tunas* players—live musicians dressed in tights, playing traditional

__Santiago, the Moorslayer__ (the Apostle James) came to Spain to preach the Bible. When King Herod killed him in Judea, his followers brought his bones back to Galicia to bury them. Eight hundred years later, when the Christians were fighting the Moors, Santiago came back to life and led the Christians to victory. The thankful Christians built a cathedral around his bones, and here it still is. Word traveled fast, and soon people from all over Europe were walking their way along the "Ruta de Santiago" to see the saint before they died. Today people drive, fly, or take the train, but the ritual honoring this patron saint of Spain is the same.

tunes for your ears only. These are usually students trying to make extra money; if you listen to them, scrape up some change.

The best time to visit Santiago is during the **Fiesta del Apóstol**, a week-long party in July honoring Santiago (St. James), the patron saint of Spain. There are bagpipe parades, giant papier-mâché figures (called *gigantes*), and performances, but the top event is the night before mass, when fireworks by the Praza Obradoira explode into a fake cathedral bonfire. Your ears may never recover.

For hundreds of years, the Spanish thought that the world ended at **Cabo de Fisterra** (Finisterre). Now you can walk out to a lighthouse and watch the waves hundreds of feet below smash into cliffs. As you face the ocean and America to your west, think about the distance that separates Europe and America, and the waves that bring them together. Brrrr!

Cantabria

Santander, Cantabria's capital city, is famous for its thirteen beautiful beaches. (Don't walk under any ladders here.) Some of the best are on the **Magdalena** peninsula, a part of Santander. But there's more to Magdalena than just beaches. Take a peek at the **Royal Palace**—now an international university. You might want to walk by the **zoo**. But as you do, keep the animals' welfare in mind. Would you want to live this far south if you were a polar bear? Past Magdalena is **El Sardinero**, the "beach town" of Santander. There's lots of beach here, and lots of people. The **Casino** has an elegant ice cream parlor for your pleasure.

When you're feeling beached out, set sail for town. On the way you'll run into the **Museo Maritim** and see the Moby Dick-size collection of whale skeletons. Another museum to dig into is the **Museo de Prehistoria**. Its Roman graves, ancient skeletons, and big bug collection are guaranteed to set your mind working. If they also

*Over 20,000 years ago, **cavemen artists** left lasting traces of their civilization: handprints, bisons, and magic symbols decorate the cave walls in animal grease and charcoal colors. The Altamira Caves probably have the most famous prehistoric paintings in the world, but you can't see them unless you're a scholar or someone who's gotten permission months ago. It's more fun to go to the **Puente Viesgo Caves** and see the real thing for yourself. Don't forget a sweater, because the cave is always chilly.*

set your stomach growling, try out some tapas at the friendly **Mesón del Toroso** on Calle Cuesta across the street from Plaza Ayuntamiento. They serve bullfight tickets here as well as yummy tortilla and other tapas. ¡Olé!

Cantabria is one of Spain's quietest areas. There are great beach towns all along the coast, a steep and snowy mountain range (the Picos de Europa), and lots of medieval towns and pre-historic caves. One of Cantabria's newest natural parks is also a free zoo. The **Parque Natural de Caberceno** lets you walk or drive around a weird rocky landscape to see lions, bears, and other creatures in their own patch of land instead of in a cage. There's also a lake with a snack bar, if you come at your own feeding time.

The streets of **Santillana del Mar** are well trodden . . . by cows, by locals, and most of all, by tourists. Still, this medieval town is fun to visit. Some of the houses here date back to the ninth century! Don't do anything until you try the yummy *bizcocho con leche* (cake and milk). You'll see signs for it everywhere.

As you cruise the cobblestone, look for coats of arms decorating the housefronts. Santillana was once the home of aristocracy. Nowadays, it's the home of farmers: you're about as likely to see a group of cows herded down the street as you are a group of tourists. To miss the busloads of these tourists, come early in the morning or, even better, stay the night.

Right outside of town is the **Zoo Santillana del Mar**. It's nothing special until you reach the Tropical Insectarium and its Butterfly Room. The insectologists keep the *mariposas* attracted with lots of sugar and flowers. See what it feels like to have hundreds of colorful butterflies fluttering around you. It's like diving into *Bambi*!

Some people think the **Costa Cantabria** has the nicest beaches in Spain. You can see the Picos de Europa mountain range on one side and the ocean on the other. If you're around, check out Gaudí's gaudy **El Capricho** palace in **Comillas**. It's now a restaurant, but unless you've got big bucks to spend for dinner, you'll probably want to head elsewhere to eat and just look here. Other nice beach towns are **San Vicente de Barqueras** and **Llanes**. Curious about those snowy peaks so close to the beach? Pack your sweater and your shades and head for the hills.

The **Picos de Europa** are one of the smallest mountain ranges in Europe, but they grow to almost 3,000 meters (10,000 feet) and have some of the best hiking anywhere. As you start uphill, you'll probably feel your ears starting to pop, so chew gum or swallow a lot. **Potes** is a touristy, last-stop-to-buy-the-groceries sort of place. If you're interested in booking mountain bike, horse, jeep, or hiking trips, you'll find lots of companies and maps to guide you.

Hold it right there! Do you like stinky blue cheese? If you do, the Picos' local cheese, Queso Cabrales, could be your idea of heaven. If you don't, hold your nose!

*Route 621 to the Picos gets really narrow and twisty at the **Desfiladero de la Hermida** (La Hermida Gorge). As a matter of fact, the walls are so high and narrow at the village of La Hermida that the town is completely in the shade between November and April. Not a good place to find sunscreen!*

The Running of the Bulls

Pamplona deserves special mention for its famous Fiesta de San Fermín. This week-long party celebrates the town's patron saint, who was martyred by being run over by bulls in the street. Every morning, six bulls are let out to run through the streets and into the bullring. Hundreds of brave (or stupid) people run in front of the bulls, taunting them while trying not to get hurt. If you hate bullfights, you'll like this. Just think of it as the bull's revenge. If you hate big crowds or miss Pamplona, visit one of the village encierros. Turismo can fill you in.

After Potes, you'll drive through some small villages and great scenery before you hit the end of the line at **Fuente Dé**. There's a parador (government hotel) here and a café. But you want to head straight for the **teleférico**. This cable car will swish you off your feet and lift you 800 meters (2,625 feet) off the ground to the top of a rock. Head for the high ledge behind the station. In summer, you'll share the mountain with lots of colorful paragliders who soar like birds through the crosswinds and scenery. You could sit and watch this forever, but you should also take a walk to see wildflowers, hear clanging cowbells, and join the group of people whose names are spelled out in stone on the ground. Plan to spend at least a couple of hours at the top of Fuente Dé; this is what the mountains are all about.

Basque Country (*País Vasco*)

While you're in Basque country, don't forget that Basques are not Spanish. They maintain that they are the only surviving native Europeans, and scholars say Basque may be Europe's most ancient language. Basques have been fighting for their independence for hundreds of years, and there's still somewhat of an ongoing war against the Spanish government. You've probably heard of **Guernica** if you've been to Madrid. On April 26, 1937, Guernica became the first civilian center in history to be the target of mass bombing. It only took four hours for the Nationalists to kill 1,600 people and completely wreck the town center. Picasso's painting made the attack infamous. The town itself is now a symbol of Basque resistance.

Because of the sometimes violent discord between Basque nationalists and the government, you're likely to see graffiti all over the walls and more police than usual. You can tell the National Police from the Basque police by the Basques' berets.

San Sebastian (Donostia, in Basque) has been a resort for over 150 years. Streets and signs are mainly bilingual or in Basque; luckily, the San Sebastian tourist map has a bilingual street index to help you along. **Playa La Concha** and its waves are the main attraction here. In fact, La Concha was named Spain's Royal Beach in 1897. You can play beachball, bodysurf, or just lie in the sun. Stands on the promenade sell necessities like sunscreen, ice cream, and water guns. Unfortunately, you'll be sharing the beach with lots of other bodies. But it's possible to find escape

routes, so don't worry! For a quick retreat, rent a kayak and paddle out to **Isla de Santa Clara** for a picnic and a swim. (There's also boat service from the port every half hour.)

The green hill of **Monte Igueldo** rises above Playa Onderatta, west of La Concha. Here you can catch not only a view of San Seb but an old-fashioned roller coaster ride at the **Parque de Attracciones** as well. Even the ride up is fun: a funicular train carries you straight up past beach villas and forest to the station.

If you were to walk all the way back down San Sebastian's lacy promenade and then follow the water, you'd pass the port on your left, a lot of seafood restaurants and souvenir shops on your right, and the **Aquarium** at the end. San Sebastian's Aquarium has hidden fish, sea turtles, whale skeletons, and fishing exhibits. If you get bored, retreat to the terrace and watch the awesome waves smash against the rocks while the windsurfers do their thing.

Past the Aquarium, take a walk along **Paseo Nuevo**, where you might get drenched from a stray wave. Gentle paths lead to the top of **Monte Urgell**. At the top, you'll find cannons still overlooking the city and lots of stony **castle ruins** to climb around on while watching people on the beach below.

San Sebastian's **Parte Viejo** is really not that old, by Spanish standards. San Sebastian has been burned down twelve times. The worst fire took place in 1813 during the Napoleonic Wars. Everything was destroyed, and the residents built this new city—what is now known as the "Old Part." There are great tapas bars in these narrow streets, and shopping for those who like it. The

Museo San Telmo is a quiet escape from the crowds. Here you'll find everything from antique Basque kitchen appliances to a cave bear skeleton and 3-D maps of the city. Finally, if you're here in August, ask about the **Fiesta Internacional de Jazz**. It's one of the best music festivals in the world.

The Pyrenees

Once upon a time, pilgrims grunted and groaned as they climbed the Pyrenees to get from Europe to Santiago. These mountains separate Spain from the rest of Europe. Now pilgrims head *to* the Pyrenees for hiking, horseback riding, paragliding, mountain biking, and skiing. And why not? They're a natural playground, with two national parks and lots of empty space to run amok in. You'll want to bring both sunscreen and sweaters, since the weather changes so quickly here, even in the summer. Adjust your attitude to the mountain altitude, take a deep breath of fresh air, and leap right in!

One of the prettiest Pyrenean valleys is the **Hecho Valley**. Hecho itself is stone old and full of creaky roofs. Just above town is a cool swimming hole with trees to play under, fish to watch, and a great rock to jump off. Don't dive! It's not that deep!

Above Hecho, you'll pass the ageless village of Siresa and then Camping Oza before you hit the end of the line. This is where the fun starts. One favorite walk is up to **Ibon Machitero**, a cirque and lake less than a kilometer from the French border. In fact, if you pass the lake, you can walk the ridge that straddles Spain and France. It's fun looking at the huge expanses of space, but don't

Andorra does not belong to either France or Spain; it's its own tiny country. Unfortunately, its main towns are more like duty-free malls than mountain paradises. The mountains nearby are nice, but it's not really worth braving the duty-free traffic from both directions.

forget to look close-up, too. You'll find salamanders, ferns, falcons, and deer comfortably at home. Before you head for the hills, make sure you have comfortable walking shoes, a good topographical map (they're available in Jaca and Hecho bookstores), and a grown-up handy. Happy hiking!

Farther east is **Ordesa National Park**, Spain's oldest national park (since 1918). If you're here in summer, just follow the string of cars to the gridlocked parking lot. Come early and bring a picnic lunch to avoid the crowds. (There's no food store, just a bad restaurant.) The best way to do the **Soaso Circle Walk** is opposite everyone else. Hit the Faja de Pelay Cliffs first, while you have the energy. Then you'll have a smooth downhill cruise for the rest of the day, and you'll be alone. Although it's crowded, this beautiful walk is worth it; don't miss the raspberry bushes on top of the cliffs or the waterfalls that glide down the valley. It's an all-day walk. If you'd rather just ramble around, take the short path to the waterfalls.

Moving east again, you'll see **Ainsa**. Although it might not look like much from the road, head directly into the old town. There's a giant plaza perfect for ice cream licking and hide-and-seek. Climb the tall, spooky tower for a cool view and a blind stairway.

The **Vall D'Aran** was created by overlapping mountains. In fact, cars couldn't even enter the valley from Spain until 1931, when a six-kilometer tunnel was built. Because of this isolation, the people here developed their own culture and language, Aranés.

Viella, at the valley entrance, is touristy and overdeveloped. But it's got a fun plaza that's perfect for watergun fights. The **Musèu dera Val D'Aran** shows what life used to be like here before cars. Another way to journey to the past is to follow the road beyond Viella, past the **Baqueira/Beret ski resort**, to the heart of the valley where you're as likely to see wild horses as German tourists. But the best way to see the Vall D'Aran is now—and always was—by foot, horse, or bike. Make arrangements and buy maps in Viella for a super-duper trip through the valley.

Another excellent trip you can take in the Pyrenees is the train called **El Cremallera**, the Zipper. It zips you past high cliffs and waterfalls, as the elevation signs go higher and higher, until you get to the valley of **Nuria**. The train was built in 1931 for Spain's first ski resort, but now it's open all year round. Just follow the river for a great walk.

6. ¡Barcelona Mès Que Mai!

Barcelona is Spain's second largest city. It's also the capital of Catalunya, Spain's most independent province. Though it's still part of Spain, people here call themselves Catalán, not Spanish. Street signs, maps, and anything else that's written will be in Catalán, not in Spanish. Luckily, almost everyone speaks both languages. Barcelona has always been a restless city. During the Spanish Civil War, it was the headquarters for opposition groups. Today, T-shirts, posters, and postcards practically shout, "¡Barcelona Mès Que Mai!" ("Barcelona More Than Ever!"), and you can almost taste the excitement. Look out when La Barça wins a soccer match!

Ramble on...and on...and on!

Barcelona's best attraction isn't a museum, a cathedral, or a ruin: it's a street! **The Ramblas**, at the heart of the city, is really five streets strung together end-to-end from Plaça Catalunya all the way down to the port. It swims with street musicians, painters, ice cream stands, fortune-tellers, jewelry sellers, pet shops, cafés, newsstands, sidewalk artists, tourists, and last but not least, Cataláns.

What's going on? The *Palau de Virreina, on the Ramblas, is the place to find out about any special concerts, plays, movies, or fiestas that will be taking place while you're in town. Another source is the* Guia de Ocio, *sold at any newsstand. It'll tell you what's playing, who's playing, and who's celebrating. And if you have any questions, don't hesitate to ask at Turismo.*

In 1992, Barcelona will be in the limelight. The city has spent over six years planning for the **1992 Summer Olympics**. They've rebuilt the 1936 Olympic Stadium on Montjuïc and renovated most of the city. If you miss the big event, you can still visit the huge stadium or take a dive into the Olympic-sized pool. With no crowds!

La Sagrada Familia

Plaça Catalunya

Picasso Museum

BARRI GÒTIC & Cathedral

ZOO

Parc de la Ciutadella

Palau de Virreina
La Boqueria
Gran Teatro del Liceu
Museu de Cera

RAMBLAS

Barceloneta

AVENIDA DEL PARALLEL

Museu Maritim

Fundació Joan Miró

Spanish Village

Amusement Park

Plaça Real & Museu de Historia Natural

Montjuïc Castle

Monument a Colom

🛈 = Tourist Information **43**

Wherever you go in Catalunya, you're sure to find people dancing the traditional Catalán sardana. They come with their own band and dance in circles. Each dancer throws a shoe or possession into the middle of the circle, showing trust in the community. Cataláns consider the sardana an expression of Catalán strength, and everyone, from children to crotchety great-aunts, dances together. Barcelona's sardanas take place every week at Plaça Catalunya, Plaça Sant Jaume, and other locations. Times and days may change, so ask about it at Turismo.

*Famed Catalán artist Joan Miró created the colorful sidewalk mosaic on the Ramblas in front of the market, **Plaça La Boqueria**. Try to find the tile where he signed his name. If you like his work, head to the Miró Foundation museum on Montjuïc.*

Plaça Catalunya is at the top of the Ramblas and the center of town. Take a seat and watch the millions of pigeons who run the show. Barcelona's biggest department store, **El Corte Inglés**, also has the best view from its top-floor cafeteria. Below you is Plaça Catalunya, to the left Montjuïc, and to the right, Tibidabo Mountain. Don't come here if you're in a hurry; the service can be slow.

Farther down the Ramblas, you'll see stands selling squawking birds, fish, turtles, and mice. Though it's fun to play, remember that pets won't be welcome on the plane home. After the bird cages, the Ramblas specialty is flowers— thousands of them in every possible color. Take time out to smell the roses during your busy day—and the daffodils, and the pansies, and the orchids.

Hungry? Even if you're not, the bustling **Mercat Sant Josep**, known locally as "La Boquería," is fun to nose around in. You'll find everything from Brie to fresh veggies to pigs' ears and rabbit. It's not like your local grocery, but it's g-r-r-eat for assembling a picnic lunch. To find bread, look for a sign saying "Forn de Pa," Catalán for "Bakery."

Escape the hustle and bustle of the city among the tiles and fountains of **Hospital de Santa Creu**. Why would you want to go to the hospital? Because it's now an art school and park. How about taking this excellent opportunity to draw in your journal?

The **Gran Teatro del Liceu** is a Ramblas landmark. If you're a music fan, take a look at the announcements posted; Liceu is a great place to see an opera, concert, or ballet. If you'd rather people-watch than hear the fat lady sing, have a seat at the **Café de la Opera** opposite the Liceu and soak up the great atmosphere. But be careful what you order; those great ringside seats come at a price.

If you're a fast food freak, you've probably spotted the McDonald's and Kentucky Fried Chicken farther down the Ramblas at Calle Ferran. But you might want to spring for *pollo asado* instead. This roasted chicken is tastier, fresher, and just as fast as fast food. Ask for a quarter chicken (*cuarto*), a half (*medio*), or the whole thing (*un pollo*). Don't forget napkins!

Little side streets from the Ramblas and Calle Ferran connect you with the **Plaça Real**. Palm trees, tourists, local kids, and the homeless make the Plaça what it is. Under the arcades you'll find cafés, tobacco stores (where you buy stamps), and a strange but free **Museu de Historia Natural** with a giant stuffed gorilla inside. On Sundays, people come from miles around to buy and sell old stamps, coins, matches, and cards. This could be the place to get a cheap, one-of-a-kind souvenir. Come between ten and three o'clock.

Below the Plaça Real, the Ramblas is littered with **souvenir shops** selling hundreds of T-shirts, stickers, hats, and everything (else) under the sun. Summer and weekend nights, there's a booming **crafts market**. But don't let shopping deter you from the **Museu de Cera**. Go ahead and explore over 300 wax beings from Don Juan to Darth Vader. If you go in for gory stuff, the upstairs is devoted to torture and famous murderers like Jack the Ripper. Yikes!

*What do you think a medieval boat factory looked like? Find out at the **Museu Maritim**. You can't miss this gigantic stone building (Drassanes) on the corner of the Ramblas and the port. Inside are boat models— from fishermen's skiffs to imperial ships. You won't see another Drassanes anywhere else, because this is the last one left. Don't miss it.*

The **Monument a Colom** marks the end of the Ramblas and the beginning of the sea. Believe it or not, you can take an invisible elevator up the base of Columbus's statue to get a fine view of the port, Ramblas, and Montjuïc. At night the statue is illuminated. If this makes you want to test your own sea legs, find a *golondrina*. These boats take you for a sightseeing spin around Barcelona's harbor. Or just meander down Passeig de Colom, following the water, the boats, and the sunset.

City Gothic . . . Got It?
The oldest part of Barcelona is called the **Barri Gòtic** (Gothic Neighborhood), and it's located east of the Ramblas. The **Cathedral** was built in 1298, almost 700 years ago. Use the side entrance and you'll enter a magical world of white geese, palm trees, sculptures, and spires. The geese are given an honorary position here because during Roman times, they saved Barcelona. Inside the Cathedral you'll see lots of stained glass and a huge *coro* (choir stalls) decorated with very familiar-looking Gothic spires.

The Barri Gòtic teems with shady streets, ancient palaces, and cafés. Open your ears and you might hear someone playing the guitar in the street. If you listen, toss them a coin. They deserve it.

In April 1493, Columbus returned to Barcelona with six natives of the New World and strange new plants, animals, and food. King Ferdinand and Queen Isabella threw a palace party for him at the **Plaça del Rei**. Enjoy a frosty cold drink while you think about the fact that it took Columbus months to get across the Atlantic and you, only a few hours.

Placa Sant Jaume has been Old Barcelona's main square since Roman times. Be careful walking, since it's still a busy city street. Three-dimensional objects will come alive in front of your eyes at **Holoscope**, Spain's first holography museum. Another fun museum in the area is the **Museu de Calzados** (Shoe Museum) in Plaça Sant Felip Neri. Inside is a collection of everything from Roman sandals to the hiking boots of the first Catalán (and Spaniard) to scale Mount Everest. Outside, examine the bullet-riddled sides of the church, left over from Spain's Civil War. It makes you stop and think.

2 Bis, at nearby Calle Bisbe, 2, is a great place to find fun gifts to take back home. Whether you're in search of a paper Sagrada Família or a flying witch, they'll have it. If silly string and fangs are more your style, head for **El Ingenio** on Calle Rauric. And definitely look at the *gigante* figures in the window.

Paleo-Christian parking!
While workers were building an underground parking lot at Plaça Seu, they bumped into something very strange. It turned out to be the remains of a fourth-century church that had been destroyed by the Moors in the tenth century. Archaeologists are busy figuring out the evidence.

Take a breather at **Plaça del Pi** (Pine Tree Square). On weekends, local artists try to sell their paintings here. Nearby **Chocolatería Dulcinea** (Carrer de Petritxol) has had Barcelona's best churros and chocolate for over a hundred years. They serve their chocolate three different ways: Spanish style (with water), French style (with milk), and Swiss style (with cream). Choose your vice.

Picasso, Santa Maria, and Snowflake

La Ribera was once a village outside Barcelona, but it got swallowed up as the city grew. The barrio is locally famous for its tapas bars. So grab a toothpick and join in the eating fun! But first, spend a few minutes with the simple glass, light, and stone of **Santa Maria del Mar** church. On a busy day, you'll enjoy the silence and calm of this beautiful building.

Are you an art fan? At the **Museu de Picasso**, you'll see the famous artist's drawings and paintings, from childhood doodles to modern works. After your art sesh, shake off any boredom at **Parc de la Ciutadella**. This used to be a fortress. Now instead of barracks there are lawns, fountains, a modern art museum, and a lake. But first you *must* meet the **Barcelona Zoo's** most famous resident, Snowflake the albino gorilla. And take a walk with a mountain goat in "Montserrat" or see a killer whale show. When you've had enough of the zoo, you'll want to explore the rest of the park.

Montjuïc, King of Mountains

Barcelona has a good reason to be proud: it was chosen to be the site of the 1992 Summer Olympics. And within the city, the focus of this great event is on the mountain of **Montjuïc** (the Jews' Mountain). But there's a lot more to Montjuïc than just the Olympic Ring of stadiums, swimming pools, and sports halls. Take the cable car ride from Barceloneta or the Columbus statue at least once. Or walk.

Up top, you can poke around the **castle** and scope out the swords and things in its military museum. Are those screams you hear? No, they're not torture victims. They're probably just fun-loving victims of the Boomerang, the **Parc d'Attraccions'** biggest roller coaster. With everything from bumper cars to candy apples to the Pasaje del Terror (an absolutely terrifying haunted house), this amusement park is guaranteed to make you smile!

Down the hill is the **Poble Espanyol** (Spanish Village). If you can't make it to all the famous buildings in Spain, this park full of replicas will show you what you're missing. It's sort of a Greatest Hits of Spain, a model town with working craftsmen. Cool yourself off at the **Mies van der Rohe Pavilion**, a German pavilion from the 1929 International Fair. Its marble pool is heaven to hot and tired feet.

On the other side of the hill are the museums. The **Fundació Joan Miró** has fun art, a great gift shop, and an outdoor sculpture roof if you start to feel claustrophobic. The **Museus Arqueològic** and **Etnològic** will fill you in on Barcelona history and world culture.

You definitely have to visit the **Palau Nacional**. The Catalán Art Museum might catch your eye, but you'll probably like the view and the fountains better. Try going at night to see the **Fonts Luminoses** (Illuminated Fountains). This is really something special. The multicolored fountains dance and sway to special music while lasers light up the sky. The shows are usually on weekend nights during the summer, but check with Turismo to avoid disappointment.

An Excellent Architectural *Eixample*

Eixample (eh-ham-pluh) means "broadening" in Catalán. This neighborhood was built in the nineteenth century when Barcelona decided to expand by knocking down its old city walls. Walk up **Passeig de Gràcia** from the Plaça Catalunya, and you'll notice that it feels different from the Barri Gòtic. Things are newer here, and more expensive. And there's a lot more space. Look down at the swirly tiles that make up the sidewalk. Between the banks and boutiques grow Alice-in-Wonderland mosaic benches begging to be used as ice cream thrones. The strangely shaped buildings on either side of you are the result of a creative period called "Modernista" that swept Barcelona in the late 1800s.

Spain's most famous architect, **Antonio Gaudí**, was the hero of this movement. Gaudí liked to use the shapes of nature and imagination in his buildings, rather than straight lines. He wanted his buildings to stand like trees, needing no support. Some of the best to keep an eye out for are **Casa Batlló**, which was designed to simulate a breaking wave, and **Casa Milà**, whose black seaweed balconies grow out of melting caveman

Getaway. . . Spend a day exploring the Monastery of Montserrat. Its ruined hermits' caves are hidden inside weirdly shaped, towering rocks. Any of the paths will take you away from the monastery to find caves, picnic spots, and strange-but-true landscapes.

51

walls. Locals call the Casa Milà "La Pedrera"— the Quarry. Both of the houses are on Passeig de Gràcia (numbers 43 and 92).

Gaudí's unfinished masterpiece, the **Sagrada Família**, is a Modernista cathedral that Gaudí thought would take 200 years to build. He worked on it for 43 years before he was run over by a streetcar. Everyone seems to disagree about how it should be finished, so work is moving slowly. Meanwhile, you can climb the 372 snail stairs all the way up the four finished towers. Along the way, you'll see great views of Barcelona, the construction, and the snails, lizards, and frogs sculpted into the stone. The breeze at the top is your reward. If you can't walk up, take the elevator and beat your friends. Back on terra firma, there's a good slide show about Gaudí; unfortunately, it's not in English.

Your favorite Gaudí creation, though, will probably be **Parc Güell**. This city park is full of weird tile balconies, funky palm-column caves, and giant lizard fountains. Bring a frisbee or a hackysack and take a break from the city. This is a great place to picnic and wander, to think and dream.

For a fantastic view and an escape from the crowds, take the funicular railway up to **Monte Tibidabo**, just north of Barcelona. When it's clear, you can see the Pyrenees in one direction and the Balearic Islands in the other. On top of the mountain is the old-fashioned amusement park, the **Parc d'Attraccions**. It may not be as big or as modern as the one at Montjuïc, but it's got a great view and some really great rides, including a 1920s aeroplane ride. Those who like to hike will find great trails around the mountain.

Barceloneta may not be the place for pristine swimming and empty sands, but Barcelona's public beach does have sun, sand, sea, and great seafood. Do go on a hunt for seaglass and shells. Don't forget your sunscreen. It gets hot here.

On the way back down (or up), don't miss the **Museu de Ciencia** near the funicular base. This is a really fun hands-on science museum where the rules say, "Please touch!"

Not far from Tibidabo is **El Laberint d'Horta**, an old topiary (hedge) maze. This is a good place to go if you feel like getting lost for a while. Before long you'll find yourself in the middle with a bunch of other previously lost people. The large park around the maze makes this a great green escape.

7. Costa Catalunya

he Costa Brava (Wild Coast) stretches from France to Barcelona. Here in the smaller towns of Catalunya you'll really see the Catalán influence. In fact, many people here never speak Spanish! The Wild Coast is not so wild anymore, thanks to some of Spain's most popular resorts. But there's plenty to do besides swim, water ski, and show off your tan!

Costa Brava South

Tossa de Mar is our first stop north of Barcelona. The **Vila Vella**, or Old Town, is surrounded by walls of gold—or so it looks when the sun is shining. Walk up and into its stony alleys from the beach. It's fun just to get lost, but at the bottom look for the **Museu Municipal**. In the basement is stuff collected from the nearby Roman ruins, and above are paintings of Tossa and the Vila Vella. In the wall opposite the museum, you can crawl through a small hole to a stone balcony overlooking a tiny beach. Go downstairs if the temptation is too great!

In the new town, the **Vila Romana** will take you back in time. Walk through the arched doorways and mosaic floors and try to imagine beach-

Cruceros are boats that cruise up and down the Costa Brava. They're expensive, but they definitely beat frying in a traffic jam.

side life in the year 200 B.C. And if all this time travel gets you hungry, don't despair. **Dino's Pizzeria**, at Calle San Telmo, 28, serves hot, cheesy pizza and great Italian food. You'll recognize Dino's by the parrot outside the door. Say cheese!

Beyond Tossa, you'll go right through beach towns such as Sant Feliu de Guixols, S'Agaro, and Platja D'Aro. The Costa Brava has some of the prettiest beaches anywhere, but heavy development has left a lot of them overshadowed by concrete apartment buildings. But don't give up the ship. Near **Calella**, you'll find great beaches, villas instead of concrete, and the **Jardines de Cap Roig**. If you've got a green thumb, you will appreciate the hard work that went into making these gardens. There's just enough shade, color, and ocean view. Don't miss the hidden castle! Nearby **Begur** towers over the countryside with its own heavily fortified castle. It's a nice walk up, and at the top you'll see beaches, plains, and even the beginning of the Pyrenees.

Spooky, Huh? If you're around Toroella de Montgri you will absolutely, positively want to see the Castell de Misteri **Magic Show**, running several times a night. You'll see a levitating piano, someone chopped in half, and other amazing feats in this mysterious old castle.

Girona

Just about everyone visiting the Costa Brava passes through Girona. But there's a lot more to it than just an airport and bus station! Like Ávila (see chapter 4), Girona is an ancient walled city. The walls were built to defend against enemies. Today you can catch a great view of the city while you stroll along its walls.

Houses perch on either side of the Riu Onyar, looking like they'll drop in at any minute. Wandering the narrow streets of Girona's **Call** (old Jewish section) is the best way to see the old town. This is the best-preserved Call in Western Europe, but don't get lost! As you walk these dark and glistening stairways, think of all the history that's taken place in these streets. Jews here, and in the rest of Spain, suffered a lot at the hands of the Christians. Finally, in 1492, they were ordered to convert to Christianity or leave the country. Learn more about Girona's Jewish history at the **Centre Isaac El Cec** (Isaac the Blind), located in the old synagogue.

Walk down Carrer de la Força, and you'll find yourself face-to-face with a giant staircase leading to Girona's **Cathedral**. Because there are no aisles, the church's interior looks bigger than it is. The Cathedral Museum is home to the famous "Creation Tapestry"—a tapestry featuring Adam, Eve, and the rest of the Garden of Eden.

See how people got clean 700 years ago at the **Banys Arabs** (Arab Baths). It's an age-old spa. For older stuff, see the **Museu Arqueològic**. It has a great collection of stuff uncovered below land and sea and an exhibit that explains underwater archaeology. Don't miss the ancient Jewish gravestones carved in Hebrew. Take a walk through the **Passeig Arqueològic**. Past the cathedral gardens, on top of the medieval walls, among the crumbling Roman ruins, you'll be walking through time. If all this ruminating on the past ruminates your stomach, head for **Caterra** on Calle Ballesteries. At this great burger joint you'll listen to 50s rock-and-roll, sit on cushy pillows, and watch the river slide by below. If you'd rather picnic, head across the river to the enormous **Parc de la Devesa**. Moss-covered fountains share the spotlight with flowers and moats in this magic spot, right near the bus and train stations.

Costa Brava North

Surrounded by pine trees, dunes, and ocean, **Empúries** is one of the prettiest ruin sites around. The town was founded by the Greeks in 600 B.C. Four hundred years later, in 195 B.C., the Romans took it over. It grew to its largest size and splendor in the first centuries A.D., then down it went, slowly but surely. Today it's in ruins, helped along by Turkish pirates in the ninth century. It's eerie walking around and thinking that the city was occupied continuously for almost 1,500 years. That's a long time!

The Greek city is really wrecked and confusing: it's hard to see more than a pile of stones. But the Roman city above has been reconstructed. You'll walk past intricate tile floors, family homes, and a grassy Roman amphitheater. Don't miss the museum store. It's got tons of projects, toys, and books for kids.

If you were to follow the backbone of the Pyrenees east, you'd end up close to **Cadaques**.

*Not only is **Empúries** Spain's most important site of Greek ruins, it's also right on the beach. If all that thinking is tiring you out, run down to the beach and swim next to the Roman breakwater, over a thousand years old.*

*Getaway. . . Drive from Cadaques to **Cap de Creus**, the easternmost point of mainland Spain. The volcanic moonscape perches above a blue, blue sea. If the wind starts getting to you, retreat inside the café—it's nice and not too expensive.*

This pretty town doesn't have a single sky-scraping hotel, yet it's one of the most popular resorts on the Costa Brava. The old town is one of Europe's trendiest areas. You'll see lots of snobby boutiques, cafés, and art galleries. At the **Museu Perrot-Moore**, take a peek at 13-year-old Salvador Dalí's chemistry book doodles. See, boring classes can be productive! Show it to your grown-up. And check out the antique truck driven by a realistic-looking Dalí and his wife. In the back are artists Miró, Picasso, and Duchamp, accompanied by the blind poet Federico García Lorca. The plaque reads, "All, it would seem, bound for a last surrealistic voyage." Cadaques was chic, even back then.

Don't forget, there's a beach here. And if you're a music lover, keep those ears open. A huge classical music festival takes place in Cadaques each August. Musicians from all over the world flock to the beach on their days off!

If you find yourself bored, burning, or both, get thee to the **Monestir de Sant Pere de Rodes**. This monastery was an important and wealthy kingdom in the Middle Ages. But in the eighteenth century, it was looted and abandoned. Today you can picnic on the shady cliffs outside the main building and savor the tasty Mediterranean view. Inside you'll find a well-restored, spooky building with lots of dark, spiral stairs leading into large, arched halls. It's the perfect, cool-down escape-from-the-beach day trip.

Figueres
The **Museu Dalí**, in Figueres, is one of the funniest and weirdest museums anywhere. Salvador Dalí is famous for his surreal art, and Figueres is

famous as Dalí's hometown. Though it doesn't contain his greatest paintings (which are owned by museums all over the world), the museum is full of some of Dalí's most imaginative sculptures. You can water plants by putting coins into a Cadillac, or walk through a life-size orchestra pit. Check out the 3-D Mae West room. You'll see the museum from afar: it's the one with the enormous eggs sitting on the roof.

Another fun Figueres museum is the **Museu de Joguets** (Toy Museum) at Rambla 10. The miniature gondola is only one of the thousands of antique toys from all over the world which are on display here.

*Getaway. . .The **Parc Natural del Delta de l'Ebre** is really for the birds. Over 250 species, to be exact. Bird lovers, kite fliers, and windsurfers will all love this wetlands area where marshes meet the sea. Skinny country roads lead to beaches, canals, and lagoons, but the best way to get around is by boat. For best results visit the Ecomuseu in the town of Deltebre first, don't wear bright clothes (they scare birds away), and get your hands on some binoculars.*

Tarragona

When you've had your fill of sun, pack up your things and head south to one of the most important cities in the Roman Empire, Tarragona. At its peak, over 250,000 Romans lived here! Imagine yourself walking through town wrapped in a toga, leather-sandaled. Running errands for the vacationing emperor, perhaps?

Spain's most interesting **Museu Arqueològic** has some great Roman exhibits, including the snakey mosaic head of Medusa and lots of headless Roman sculptures. And the basement gift store has some excellent postcards and posters. Next door, in the Roman Palace, is the **Museu Historic**. Peer into the tunnels to the Roman Circus. These tunnels were escape routes for royalty if war broke out! Climb to the top terrace and towers for a kingly view over the city.

For a change of pace, walk along the **Rambla Nova**, a smaller version of Barcelona's Ramblas. This clean and shiny walk is heaven for skateboarders and rollerskaters. At its end is the **Balcón del Mediterráneo**, where you can see the Roman amphitheater, the beach, and, of course, the Mediterranean. If you walk downstairs and keep the water on your left, you'll come to Tarragona's port, El Sollér. Past the rusty freighters and palm trees are crowded seafood restaurants serving Tarragona's specialty, pescado romesco (fish with romesco sauce). Walk around the docks to build up your appetite—there will still be some people fishing, lots of little fish in the water, and boxes stacked up ready for tomorrow's auction. Then hit **La Puda**'s crowded terrace. Yum!

In 1923, the Arrendataria Tobacco Company began construction of a new factory on the outskirts of town. Much to their surprise, they began digging up ancient graves and skeletons. You, too, can see the **Necropolis**, where both Christian and pagan tombs are on display. There are even a few skeletons lying around!

One of Tarragona's best sights is outside of the city itself. The **Puente del Diablo** (Devil's Bridge) is a Roman aqueduct that stretches for over 200 meters through the woods. You can find it by following the road to Barcelona, but keep your eyes peeled. There's parking on the side of the road; you have to hike in to see this amazing, overgrown water bridge.

*Killer Croissants! If you prefer croissants to catacombs, find your way to **Café Mel i Mata** on Calle Mayor and sample the world's best chocolate croissants.*

8. A Wind from the East

Warning! *Beware of old maps that call Plaza Ayuntamiento "Plaza de País Valenciano."*

Southeast Spain is sometimes called the Levante (which means East), and it is Europe's most fertile stretch of land. La Levante will keep you busy with castles, caves, and fireworks fiestas. When you've had enough of exploring, collapse onto the nearest beach and soak up the rays. And if your stomach starts to growl, pig out on paella, a concoction of rice, saffron, meat or chicken, and seafood. Valencia is famous for this dish, so dig in!

Valencia and Around
Valencia is Spain's third largest city, after Madrid and Barcelona. Even though it's big, most of what you'll want to see is in a circle around the old city. **Plaza Ayuntamiento** is named for its *ayuntamiento*, or town hall. Look for the giant bat on top of the building; bats are Valencia's mascot and good-luck symbol. (Where's Herman Munster?) Get a map at Turismo, and then make your way inside to the small **Museo Histórico**. Here you'll find, among other things, heavy storybook keys to the city, Jaime I's 66-pound shield and sword, and town records dating back to the 1400s.

Southeast Spain

Map labels: Castellón de la Plana, Sagunto, Valencia, Alzira, La Albufera, Gandía, Denia, Xativa, Guadalest, A7, Jijona, Benidorm, Alicante, Coves de Can Jobre, Murcia, Elche, Tabarca Island, 301, Costa Blanca, Cartagena

Wander up Calle San Vicente to the **cathedral**. You'll see the huge **Miguelete** tower from far away. If you climb all 203 stairs, your reward will be a killer view of the city. Try to count the blue-domed churches below. Duck into the Cathedral Museum's chapel for a peek at what some say is the **Holy Grail**—the cup Jesus Christ is supposed to have used at the Last Supper. Many have searched for it, including Monty Python and Indiana Jones. This cup *was* hidden away for centuries in remote corners of mountainous Aragon. What do you think?

*Like explosions? You won't be alone in Valencia. In March, the city erupts in celebration of **Las Fallas**. Neighborhoods all over the city build elaborate floats, and after days of parades, bullfights, and fireworks, all the floats are burned in a giant bonfire at the same time. Valencianos say that they are burning up all the bad luck for the year ahead. You can see much smaller versions of these ill-fated floats at Valencia's **Museu de Fallas**, a bus ride or drive away from the city center.*

*Valencia was occupied by the Moors for over three hundred years until the famous warrior **El Cid** captured it in 1094. He died five years later, but the Moors were still scared off when his dead body was propped onto a horse and led through the gates. The Moors recaptured the city in 1101, but Jaime I of Aragon recaptured it for good in 1238, and it's been Catholic ever since.*

Your quest for the Holy Grail may soon turn into a quest for ice cream. When this happens, head for Plaza Santa Catalina. Here you'll find crowds enjoying ice cream, chocolate, and horchata at **Horchatería Santa Catalina** and **El Siglo**, both of which have been scooping out desserts for over a hundred years. Just around the corner from these lickeries is Plaza Redonda, which doubles as a **flea market** during the day. You'll find anything and everything from antique tiles to the latest jeans here. If you're in the market for food, head to **Mercado Central**. This humongous market is absolutely crawling with fresh food. What's that? You say you don't like eating still-crawling snails for lunch? You'll just have to settle for a freshly picked orange, then. Too bad, huh? As you munch on your snails (I mean orange), slip into **La Lonja**. For hundreds of years, this was one of the most important stock exchanges in Spain. As you can see, things were a bit calmer back then.

Right near the cathedral is the **Ceramics Museum**, housed in the **Palacio del Marques de Dos Aguas**. (Try saying *that* ten times fast!) Hipolito Rivera, the architect, went crazy decorating this building. Literally. When he was finished, he went insane.

Beyond the cathedral at the outside of the old city are the **Torres de Serrano**, one of the original gates to the city. Look at it from both sides; the Valencia gates were designed to show a fierce face to outsiders while remaining civil to citizens. Bookworms will be relieved to find **Librería Inglesa**, an English-language bookstore down the street. You'll find everything from comic books to horror and sci-fi here. On your way back toward the cathedral, cool out with a *corte gigante*: a giant scoop of ice cream crunched between two wafers. Yummmmmm.

Across the river park from the Torres de Serrano is Valencia's largest existing park,

*Getaway. . .The first thing you'll see when you get to **Morella** is its huge castle built into a rock cliff. This fortress town has seen its share of battles. You could spend hours exploring all the nooks and crannies of the ruined castle and hours more watching the birds that swoop around its sunshiny edges. If you're here in August, don't miss the **Fiestas de Agosto**, with a small running-of-the-bulls. Just stay out of the way. Farther south, near the town of Vall de Uixó, ride the underwater river into the center of the earth at the **Grutas de Sant Josep**. It's a cave rave.*

Jardines del Real. Besides offering lots of welcome shade, these royal gardens are home to a small **zoo** and an important museum, the **Museo de Bellas Artes**.

Inside the museum you'll first come across archaeological treasures like the Roman mosaic of a centaur attacking a tiger. Upstairs are Gothic primitives, which may seem pretty boring until you realize that they were really early comic books for illiterate Spanish peasants. A third floor has more modern paintings, and up top you'll find a room full of GIGANTIC paintings. Don't miss it. And remember, if you're bored, you can always meet your grown-up outside in the park.

The Torres de Quart are city gates like the Torres de Serrano. Just beyond them you'll find Valencia's **Jardí Botànic**, a fantastic collection of flowers, plants, insects, and butterflies from all over the world. Around the corner is a brand-new modern art museum, the **Centro Julio Gonzalez**.

Valencia's **bullring** is right next to the train station. Through the mall entrance next door is the **Museo de Taurino**, Spain's oldest bullfight museum, dating from 1929. Matadors' outfits hang inches away from famous bulls' heads. It makes you want to see them dance to the "típico" Spanish music they play overhead.

The Gran Vía stretches from the bullring all the way to the Turia River Park. Though its official name is **Gran Vía Marques del Turia**, it could easily be nicknamed "Avenue of the Americas." Walking down the wide, shady island, you'll run into **Foster's Hollywood** restaurant, **Pizza Hut, VIPs, Kentucky Fried Chicken**, and, as a grand finale, **7 Eleven**. What country are we in?

Back in Black! *Every Thursday at noon, crowds gather to watch the **Tribunal de las Aguas** in action. These famous judges have been appointed to dress in important-looking black robes and discuss the regional water irrigation system in public. They've been doing it for centuries, and they look it.*

The Gran Vía ends at the finished section of the **Turia River Park**. This wide green expanse is a great place to toss a frisbee or kick a soccer ball. The great glass building you see in front of you is Valencia's brand-new **Palau de Musica**. Look for its reflection in the shallow reflecting pool (what else is a reflecting pool for?). There are sometimes free concerts here, so check out the schedule. And if you can, see the music palace lit up at night. It's beautiful.

Just south of Valencia is the pine tree-lined beach of **El Salér**. You may have to fight the crowds at first, but it's a nice long beach with plenty of room to the sides.

Near El Salér is **La Albufera**, a large lagoon separated from the sea by a sandbank and surrounded by rice fields. This is one of Spain's largest bodies of fresh water, and it attracts thousands of birds—about 250 species. It's recently been made a Natural Park and, being so close to Valencia, is a nice place to go for half a day. The best way to see La Albufera is by boat. Just look for handpainted signs along the road. There's a good chance that your guides will be the same age as you, using their family fishing boat. They'll point out storks, wild ducks, and other birds that live here as you drift through the lagoon and narrow canals. If you're lucky, you'll catch the sunset.

The Costa Blanca, More or Less

Gandía's beach is long and silky, its horchata icy cool. Head north to the beach dunes—a great place for frisbee. You can walk there on the beach or seaside paseo if you've got the time and energy.

Denia, farther along the coast, was named by

*For hundreds of years, the Turia River flowed above and around Valencia. Then it dried up. Now landscape architect Ricardo Bofill is turning the entire river bottom into one of the **world's biggest parks**. So far, only a couple of sections have been converted, but when it's finished—look out, world!*

the Greeks after Diana, goddess of the hunt. Today you can see some of the stuff they left behind at the fun and informative **Museu Arqueològic**. There's a room for each culture that lived here: Greek, Roman, Moorish, and Christian. To get to the museum, wind your way up the crumbling ramparts of the castle. Become an explorer!

South of Denia the towns and beaches get smaller and rockier. But rocky is an understatement for **Calpe**. It's famous for the **Peñon de Ifach**, an enormous rock jutting out into the ocean. Nothing beats getting to the top of the Peñon, but make sure you're prepared. Wear good shoes (sneakers are okay), and don't carry anything in your hands. You'll need them for scrambling. You'll want to keep a grown-up handy, too. Start early and give yourself lots of time, if you don't want your blood to boil over. It'll take you half a day round-trip.

From the Peñon de Ifach you can see the huge concrete sprawl of **Benidorm**, one of the Mediterranean's biggest resorts. It's a lot like Miami Beach—hard to find the sand underneath all the tourists and tall buildings. But don't miss nearby **Aqualandia**, a great water park filled with Kamikazes, Rapids, Zig-Zags, and other fun water rides. You must be at least 1.25 meters (4 feet) tall for some of the rides.

Beached out? Rest in **Guadalest**. Besides its mountain scenery, Guadalest has a very special attraction: the **Mundo de Max** museum of miniatures. Professor Max spent over 30 years traveling to all corners of the globe. This is one of two places where you can see what he brought back with him (the other is in Mijas, Andalucía, chapter 9): a bird carved on a matchstick, pin-head portraits, dressed up fleas, and more. In fact, some of the items are so small you'll have to look through a microscope to see them. They say the world is getting smaller, but this is ridiculous.

Outside Alicante

Before you reach Alicante there are two great side trips to take. The first is to the **Coves del Canelobre**. Descend into these 110-million-year-old caves with a sweater—it's always 15°C (59°F) down here. You'll see formations that look like castles, coral, silk, bamboo, and monster brains. The central cave is called the cathedral, because the acoustics are perfect—no echo in any direction.

All that exertion may make you hungry. You'd better head to **Jijona** right away for a look at its *turrón*—or nougat—factories. The best one to visit is **Turrón El Lobo** (The Wolf). The aroma of cooking candy greets you at the door and follows you through the factory. Try to ignore it as you learn that the factory was founded in 1725 and look at its collection of antique candy molds, machinery, and costumes. Maybe you'll be able to see the factory workers actually making the candy. The sweet smell of almonds and honey will undoubtedly grow stronger here. Pay no attention as you discover that they make over 1,800 tons of *turrón* here per year. Just when you think you can't stand any more, the tour is over and it's taste-test time. Finally!

Alicante

At the heart of Alicante is a wavy waterfront paseo called the **Explanade de España**. The sidewalk cafés can be expensive, but you can always hang out at the McDonald's and Burger King tables for cheap. Or just sit in one of the brightly colored chairs and watch the parade of people and pigeons. At night there's a crafts market here with everything from Moroccan drums to Peruvian whistles.

If you think you don't like modern art, the **Museo de Arte de Siglo XX** might change your mind. Aim for the second floor, where you'll find optical illusions and a space pod.

The **Castello de Santa Barbara** is probably the easiest castle to get to in the world. All you have to do is step into an elevator across from the beach. The elevator shaft goes right through the huge hunk of rock that the castle stands on. You'll probably meet the friendly cats who live on the towers. Explore the castle with them at your heels.

Tabarca Island

If you've got a hankering for island life, head for the harbor. Several boats a day leave Alicante for

During the first two weeks of August, the town of Elche re-creates battles between the Christians and the Moors. Watch the elaborately dressed sòldiers duke it out until the Moors are forced out of the city.

the Isla de Tabarca, a tiny island only an hour away, now protected as a marine reserve. As you break away from the harbor, you'll have a great look at the castle and of Alicante's coast-hugging high-rises. On Tabarca, you're in another world. If you have snorkeling gear you'll be in heaven; if not, you can take glass-bottom boat trips in season. Wander away from the beach to see what Tabarca is really like: dirt streets, sleeping dogs, secretive cats, and a friendly general store (*tienda*). There are seafood restaurants lining the beach, but fish-haters will definitely want to bring a picnic lunch from Alicante. You can also reach Tabarca from Santa Pola and Torrevieje.

Elche

The town of Elche, southwest of Alicante, is famous for its palm trees. Over 400,000 of them, to be exact. This is the largest **palm forest** in all of Europe. You can see them for free in the Municipal Park, but if you want to see rarities like the imperial 8-legged palm, you'll have to visit the **Huerta del Cura**, a private garden. Elche is the linguistic frontier of Spain; south of here people speak Spanish, not Catalán.

9. The South: Moors, Mountains, and More

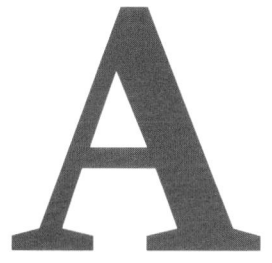

ndalucía is the Spain most people expect to see: bullfights, bright colors, gypsies, and white-washed villages. But it's also got spooky caves, old movie sets, and some of Europe's highest mountains. The Moors controlled some parts of Andalucía for over 700 years. In fact, they were the wealthiest and most advanced civilization of the Middle Ages. Their influence can still be seen today, and not just in Spain. Ever hear of algebra, paper, arabic numerals, or irrigation canals? All were introduced by the Moors. Granada's magnificent Alhambra and the grand mosque in Córdoba will make you think about the Islamic royalty who inhabited Spain for so long.

Moorish mathman? Some people say that the Giralda tower was built by the same man who invented algebra. He built the ramps in a spiral so that two horsemen could pass each other. He also invented your homework. Thanks a lot, dude!

Sevilla and Around

Don't forget to wear a hat and drink lots of water while you're in Spain's sunniest and most magical city. **Sevilla** was the Moors' stronghold after the Moorish capital, Córdoba, crumbled. When the Christian army surrounded the town in 1247, they didn't expect the Moors to fight for over a year. It was the toughest battle of the Reconquest, and when it was over, the Chris-

tians were amazed by the beautiful city they found inside.

In 1402, the new Catholic rulers of Sevilla decided that they needed to make their mark. "Let us put up a building of such immense proportions," they said, "that the rest of the world will think us mad." And they did. They demolished the mosque and built the largest **Gothic cathedral** in the world. It only took a hundred years, which might seem long but which is peanuts for cathedral building. The only part of the mosque they left standing was the **Giralda** tower. The Moors had used the tower

The South

Portugal

Córdoba

Italica

Jaén

Sevilla

Guadix

Huelva

Granada

COTO DOÑANA NATIONAL PARK · Setenil · Antiquera LAS ALPUJARRAS

Jerez de la Frontera · Cádiz

CUEVA DE LA PILETA · Ronda · Torremolinos · Almuñecar · Almería

Marbella · Mijas · Málaga

El Cabo de Gato

Tarifa · Gibraltar

COSTA DEL SOL

Ceuta

Tangier · Morocco

for prayer calling, but the Christians turned it into a bell tower. Circle your way to the top. What a view!

Around the corner is the **Alcázar**, or Moorish Palace. When you're done investigating royal Moorish life-styles, the garden in back will reward you (look for the fish pond).

Behind the "Big Three" (Giralda, Cathedral, Alcázar) you'll find the **Barrio Santa Cruz** and its whitewashed alleys, flowers, and touristy restaurants. The tall, narrow streets were designed to keep out the torturous sun, and most of them are too skinny for cars. Look for hidden plazas in this area.

The **Plaza de España** was originally planned for the 1929 Fair of the Americas (it went broke in the Depression). Wander along the half-moon paseo and inspect the 50 tiled benches. The scenes represent every province from Albacete to Zaragoza! Over the bridge and across the street, you'll find shady **Maria Luisa Park**, a perfect place to read, relax, and shake off your sightseeing blahs.

EXPO 92, the World's Fair, will commemorate the 500th anniversary of Columbus's voyage to the Americas. Over 18 million people are expected to come (between April and October 1992), and more than 200 countries will be participating with exhibits ranging from antique to out-of-sight futuristic. When it's all over, you can tour the site and see some of the nutty buildings that different countries have built.

¡Oye! Flamenco is the music of Andalucía, and Sevilla is the flamenco capital of Spain (and the world!). One of the best places to see a show is at "Los Gallos" (The Roosters) at Plaza Santa Cruz in the Santa Cruz Barrio, near the cathedral. Swaggering singers, daring dancers, and gitano (gypsy) guitarists will have you clapping along.

Two of Spain's largest fiestas happen in Sevilla: **Semana Santa** *(the week before Easter), which is celebrated all over Spain, and the* **April Feria**, *a week-long market festival full of music, dance, and food. If you're around, don't miss either of these exciting celebrations!*

Figaro, Figaro, Fi . . ga . . ro! Four famous operas have been set in Sevilla: The Marriage of Figaro, Carmen, Don Giovanni, *and (of course)* The Barber of Seville.

Another good place to cool out is Paseo de Cristobal Colón, on the Guadalquivir River. Look for the **Torre de Oro** (Tower of Gold), which used to hold the Moorish and Christian kings' gold loot. Now it just holds a small navy museum. Make like Columbus and row toward the New World, or check out Spain's oldest bullring, **La Maestranza**, built between 1760 and 1763. It's just off of the Paseo, a short walk away.

Near Sevilla lie the Roman ruins and mosaics of **Italica**, just outside Santiponce. After the Romans were defeated, it was abandoned (the Visigoths liked Sevilla better). Wander the ancient streets and look for the **mosaics** that decorated early homes. Don't miss the ruins of its enormous **amphitheater**, either; it's the third largest in the world. You can still see the seats, corridors, and dens for the hungry lions! Will the Astrodome survive this long?

Córdoba

Córdoba was once the capital of Moorish Spain and the largest and richest city in Europe. Its **Mezquita** is the largest and most beautiful Moorish mosque ever built. It stands right in the heart of the city, guarding the old quarter. If you enter the mosque through the Patio de las Naranjas (Orange Tree Patio), you'll see how the inside mimics the outside. Over a thousand different columns support the building. These pillars were recycled from Greek, Roman, and Visigothic ruins, and some of them even came from as far away as Carthage and Constantinople. No two are alike. Find a quiet place and examine this incredible forest.

Not far from the mosque is Córdoba's **Museo Taurino**, with a large collection of bull's heads. Behind it is the "**Zoco**," where the Moorish market used to be. Today it's a great place to watch crafts-people of every sort work on their projects. And if you see something you like, well, maybe you'll have a handmade souvenir of Spain.

If you want to know more about the Moors who lived here, cross the Roman bridge to the Torre de la Calahorra. Inside is the incredibly cool **Living Museum of Andalucía**. By strapping on a pair of cordless headphones you'll see and hear moving models of history in four languages (including English). Don't miss seeing a day and night of Granada's Alhambra (a model, of course), complete with music.

Granada and Around

Granada was so sacred to the Moors that they still include it in their nightly prayers to Allah. It's been called a Mountain Eden. All because it's

Getaway. . .Coto Doñana National Park, south of Sevilla, is one of Europe's biggest stretches of wilderness. The park can only be seen by guided Land Rover tour. In four hours you'll see eagles, flamingoes, deer, wild boar, and maybe other animals (mountain lions have occasionally been spotted). Before you embark (at the Centro de Recepción del Acebuche), walk around the natural history exhibit so you know what you're in for. Park tips! Call ahead, take the morning trip, and rent binoculars at the center.

*Córdoba is famous for its patios, which make cool and airy living rooms during the hot summer. During May, a **Patio Festival** is held, and people compete to decorate their patios most outlandishly.*

Rust never sleeps. Or does it? Sultan Abu'l-Hasan murdered sixteen of his sons in the Hall of the Abencerrages so that his son Boabdil could become sultan. Legend has it that the rusty spots in the fountain are really indelible spots of their blood.

the home of the **Alhambra**. This huge Moorish palace is one of the most beautiful in the world. Drift your way through its pools, courtyards, fountains, arches, and orange trees. You'll enjoy it most if you miss the huge tour groups, so start when it opens and skip the Alcazaba, or visit during lunchtime. Soak up the mysterious atmosphere of the Court of the Lions, the Hall of the Abencerrages, and the Royal Baths, where light was refracted through star-shaped holes to create a rainbowy tub. Hear for yourself the strange "whisper effect" in the dark and gloomy Chapel Crypt. And if you're ever tired, stretch out on the comfy leather chairs and imagine yourself sultan of the Middle Ages' greatest civilization.

Near the Alhambra is the **Generalife**, or summer palace. Admission is included with your Alhambra ticket. The gardens follow the Koran's descriptions of heaven, full of the sacred substance of life, water. You'll find plenty of colorful and secret spots to hide in here.

Don't forget, your ticket to the Alhambra can and should be split over the course of a few days. *No one* could see everything here in one day; it's silly even to try.

In town, marvel at Ferdinand and Isabella's **Capilla Real** (Royal Chapel). During their reign they used almost a quarter of the royal income to build this, their final resting place. But their own tombs couldn't be simpler—just iron caskets behind bars.

Walk up the cobbly Caldereria Nueva to the old Moorish quarter, the **Albaicin**. But first make an Arabic pit stop on this street for yummy crepes, chocolate, or lunch. Mmmm! You'll probably see Arabic graffiti here. After you walk around the Albaicin, catch the sunset from **San Nicolas Church**. You'll find the Sierra Nevada mountains glowing red behind the Alhambra.

You may be tempted to head up to the **Sacramonte gypsy caves** at night. This is one of the biggest tourist ripoffs in Europe, but it's fun seeing the caves. If you decide to go, don't bring any valuables and *do* bring a grown-up. Gypsies are discriminated against in Spain, so they sometimes steal to make a living. It's sad but true. If you just want to see the caves, try walking up here during the day. You'll be harassed less this way.

Nice altitude! *The Veleta road into the Sierra Nevada (Snowy Mountains) is Europe's highest navigable road—at least in August! At other times of the year, you'll have to hike to get to the top. Keep your eyes peeled for wildflowers and horned mountain goats hiding in the landscape. Solynieve has skiing from November to May, which means that in spring you can ski one day and lie on the beach the next. Radical!*

Lights, Camera, Action! If you're a movie buff, you'll be interested to know that part of Indiana Jones and the Last Crusade *was filmed in Guadix. You'll also want to head toward* **Yucca City/Mini Hollywood**, *where over 200 spaghetti westerns were once shot. Ride through town, saunter through the saloon, or get yer picture taken in frontier duds. Nearby* **El Cabo de Gato** *is a great place to bed down. Its deserted beaches and friendly people are perfect for tired banditos and vaqueros (cowboys) needing a good swim.*

East of Granada

Guadix is known for its amazing **cave barrio**. Believe it or not, half of the town's population lives here. Most of the caves not only have running water and electricity but even second stories, VCRs, and satellite dishes. But in the deeper parts of town, some people still live in caves with just chimneys and doors attached. It's like being let loose on the Flintstones set, minus Dino and plus mules.

Las Alpujarras is a collective name for the villages of the southern Sierra Nevada, facing the sea. This is how Spain used to be: old men riding mules to work, widows dressed in black, and not a skyscraper to be found. Visit **Global Turismo** in Pampaneiro or Bubión. These friendly environmentalists can arrange trips by horse, mule, foot, mountain bike, snowshoe, ski, or rock. If you'd rather just explore on your own, get a good topographical map. Most towns have a weaving workshop you can visit. Ask around for the *talleres de tejidos.*

The Costa del Sol

The Costa del Sol covers Spain's southern coast. It's one of the most famous beach resort areas in the world, which is another way of saying it's packed with hotels. But there's a lot of fun to be had here: on the beach, at amusement parks, and on trips inland to the rest of Andalucía.

Most people pass through **Málaga** to get to where they're staying. After all, it is the Costa del Sol's biggest city. But before you leave, take the time to walk through the gardens of the **Alcazaba** to the **Archaeological Museum** housed inside the fortress's walls. You'll find interesting Moorish artifacts and a hair-raising view of the beautiful coast and hideous high-rises. Try to spot the **cathedral**'s unfinished tower; a Málaga bishop gave away his tower money to support the American Revolution. What a guy.

West of Málaga, the Costa del Sol really gets going with hotels and high-rises. People from all over the world vacation here; you're as likely to see a banker from Texas as you are a rock star from London or a manicurist from Stockholm. One of the strangest resorts is **Torremolinos**. There's not much to do in this tacky town but go to the crowded beach and watch sunburned tourists walking around. And shop anywhere and everywhere.

In fact, you'd better take off for **Tivoli World**, an enormous amusement park. From roller coasters to Mouseville to an Andalusian square with flamenco shows, there's not much that this fun *parque de attracciones* misses. If your head is swimming with heat, head to **Aquapark**, which has lots of water fun and a Treasure Island miniature golf course.

Trevelez, *at 1,476 meters, is Spain's highest inhabited town. Its riverbanks are perfect for a high-class picnic.*

Attention Scotland Yard!
Torremolinos has an unusually high concentration of British criminals. Because Britain formerly had no extradition agreement with Spain (which meant the British police could not come take British criminals back to England for trials), many famous criminals, including one from the Great Train Robbery, now live in or around this crowded beach city.

Getaway. . . El Torcal National Park is only a half hour from Antequera. Use your imagination and its strangely shaped rocks will transform themselves into Darth Vader, Twin Towers—anything but plain old stone! Follow the paths marked by arrows so you don't get lost.

Not far from Tivoli World is **Mijas**, where the most popular mode of transport (for tourists at least) is **mule taxi**. You'll feel like a million bucks riding around in one. The best spot to aim for is the **Carramoto de Max** miniatures museum. Professor Max traveled for over 30 years collecting the smallest things in the world. You'll peer through magnifying glasses at costumed fleas and *The Last Supper* painted on a grain of rice. You'll even see someone's shrunken head from the Amazon. Gross! Professor Max has another museum in Guadalest (see chapter 8).

Join the beautiful people in a stroll down **Marbella**'s seafront promenade, or just hang out at one of the beaches. Either way, you're bound to get wet. Marbella is the Costa's wealthiest town, with more Rolls Royces than anywhere else but London. Chances are that most of these high rollers really live in **Puerto Banus**, the nearest yacht marina. It's fun to walk through the marina and see the extra-deluxe sailboats and motor yachts moored here. But, be careful— prices here are extra-deluxe, too!

White Towns and Around

Antequera is a small town with a good idea: they've turned their ruined **castle** into gardens that are fun to explore. You'll get a fantastic view of the town and mountains from here. You'll also be able to see the **Cueva de Manga** way off in the distance. This cave and a few others like it were burial tombs for ancient Iberians who lived here thousands of years ago. The roof of the Cueva de Manga is a 180-ton slab of rock that archaeologists think was dragged over five miles and then hoisted on top of the building. Early bodybuilders?

Ronda is split in half by a yawning river gorge spanned by three stone **bridges**. One is Roman, one is Moorish, and the most impressive, called the **Puente Nuevo** (New Bridge), dates from 1735. The Puente Nuevo connects the old town with the new town. In summer, you can have a snack at the bar that sits in the middle of the bridge (if you're not afraid of heights). Just forget that this used to be the jail during the Spanish Civil War and that some prisoners were actually thrown into the gaping gorge below as their punishment. Gulp! Every May, "Goya" bullfights take place in eighteenth-century costume in Ronda's bullring, one of the oldest in Spain.

Setenil's streets are called *cuevas* because they're protected overhead by ledges, which are also floors of people's houses. Cross the bridge and head for the crumbling tower above town for a nice walk and an excellent view.

Farther away from Ronda is the **Cueva de la Pileta**, a series of caves with Neolithic paintings of animals, fish, and what anthropologists think are magic symbols. This is an archaeological site, not a tourist attraction, so you won't see any cheesy colored lights. Just the flicker of a lantern and the colors of early graffiti artists. José Antonio Bullon, whose grandfather discovered the caves, speaks a little English and his sign-language is impeccable. Don't miss his tour.

Are you an eagle eye? On your way to Ronda, look for imperial eagles wheeling in the drafts above you. The spectacular birds thrive in the dry mountains surrounding the town.

*The famous **Andalusian Riding School** in Jerez de la Frontera has shows every Thursday at noon where the horses and riders parade around performing impossible tricks in unbelievable costumes. (Kind of like the Three Amigos.) But you may have more fun on other days, when you can see the riders practicing and the horses up close.*

83

The Southern Tip

The **Rock of Gibraltar**, known locally as "Gib," may take you by surprise. Bet you didn't expect to find bobbies, fish-and-chips, or the changing of the guard in España! This may be the last remaining British colony, but people here speak Spanish as often as English. Still, it's strange making your way down Main Street after all the calles and avenidas you've been navigating.

Near the end of Main Street, look for the **cable car** that goes to **Top of the Rock**. And prepare yourself for an unbelievable view. Across the Strait of Gibraltar are Morocco's Atlas Mountains. Yes, that's how close you are to Africa. If you walk down you'll pass **Apes Den**, the home of Europe's last remaining (though tail-less) monkeys. Legend has it that as long as the monkeys survive, Gibraltar will remain in British hands. Not far from here is the path to **St. Michael's Cave**. The cave is so deep that the Romans thought it was a bottomless pit. Also on the Rock is the **Tower of Homage**, a ruined Moorish castle. The British flag has flown here since 1704, when the Spanish were defeated.

The **Gibraltar Museum** has a replica of the first Neanderthal skull ever found and a great scale model of the Rock. You'll learn why the Spanish border was closed to the people of Gibraltar between 1969 and 1985 and everything had to travel by boat or plane. For once, the labels are in English.

It's easy to go to Africa from here, or from smaller and nicer **Tarifa**, the southernmost point of Spain. This was nowheresville until windsurfers discovered it in the early 1980s. Now it's *the* surf spot of Europe. Come here if only to check out the radical surfers doing their thing in the wind. But beware: the wind is great for windsurfers and awful for beachsitters. Snoop the tiny streets of the old town and climb around on the castle's crumbly ramparts to see Africa only seven miles across the water. Then visit it.

How? By taking a day trip to **Morocco**. Tours leave for Tangier just about every day. These crowded bus tours hit the famous camel-ride stop, a restaurant, and then go shopping all day. If you're more adventurous, you can go on your own and hire an official guide at the port, but be careful, especially in Tangier. Like any border town, it's got its share of hustlers and creeps. If you really want to see Morocco, you'll have to stay overnight and go beyond Tangier. Make sure your grown-up has a good guidebook.

No matter how or where you go, prepare yourself for something different. Morocco is definitely the Third World. No matter what, you will seem incredibly rich to most people, so get ready to be harassed. Everything looks, smells, and sounds different, from veiled market women to loud drum-playing Arabs in the narrow steps. You'll have plenty of opportunity to buy souvenirs—in fact, you'll have to push vendors out of your way. Be prepared to bargain. On the way back, you can talk about what a different experience this has been.

10. A Slice of Island Life

The Balearic Islands lie off Spain's eastern coast, near Valencia and Alicante. The three biggies are Mallorca, Menorca, and Ibiza. They're all fun in their own way. And, of course, they've all got great beaches, so if all you want to do after all this exploring is go swimming, sailing, or water-skiing you've come to the right spot! Don't forget that they don't speak Spanish here, they speak a dialect of Catalán or English.

Mallorca

Mallorca is the largest and best-known Balearic island. Though it attracts millions of tourists from all over the world, most of Mallorca is not resort. The tourists flock to the **Bay of Palma** with its big hotels, crowded beaches, and expensive restaurants. But there's much more to Mallorca than sun, sea, and shopping.

Most people pass right through Palma's airport or ferry port on their way to a hotel. Don't take off so fast! If you're feeling flush, take a ride through the old town in a horse-drawn carriage. Just plain walking is fun, too. Palma's **cathedral** has rainbow lights inside, thanks to Catalán

Mallorca

Puerto de Pollença · Pollença · Sa Calobra · Artá · Puerto de Soller · Inca · Porto Cristo · Soller · Petra · Manacor · Deya · Banyalbufar · Palma de Mallorca · Llucmayor · Felanitx · Bay of Palma · El Arenal

Mediterranean Sea

architect Gaudí. Next door, you'll find the **Palacio Almudaina**, where they give some pretty funny tours in English, French, German, and Spanish. Have an ice cream at the **Plaza Mayor** and poke around its crafts market. Near Palma is El Arenal, with lots of beach, tourists, high-rises, and the **Bellver Castle** to explore.

Take the train from Palma to **Soller** just for the ride, as it dips through mountains and valleys on its narrow track. You'll pass olive and almond groves that are nearly a thousand years old. At Soller, get on the wooden tram that will take you down to **Puerto de Soller**. This is the home base

*On Mallorca, try chomping down on **Pa-amb-oli** instead of an ordinary bocadillo. These local sandwiches are made with bread rubbed with tomato and olive oil. Yummm.*

California dreaming? You may have heard about Fray Junípero Serra in school. This Spanish priest founded famous California missions—the roots of San Diego, San Francisco, and many other towns. Why California? Maybe it's because this island boy grew up on Mallorca and yearned for sunshine. Visit his house and museum in his hometown, Petra.

Sa Granja in Mallorca is a fun open-air museum where you can see how people lived hundreds of years ago, hear their music, watch them dance, and even eat the same kinds of donuts (buñuelos) as they did! See, kids weren't so different then, after all.

for some really fun boat trips. Local kids say the best trip is to Sa Calobra, but you'll have a good time on any of them.

South of Puerto de Soller is the stone village of **Deya**. You might hear lots of American, British, and German voices in Deya: it's the unofficial expatriate hometown of Mallorca. There's a great pizzeria here and an even better beach, **Cala Deya**. To get down to it, you'll have to take the long road or the shorter (but steeper) dirt path. Walk along the cliff path from Cala Deya and see how far you can get.

The northwest coast of Mallorca is full of tall mountains—nothing like the other islands. If you don't take the boat trip, then at least drive down the curvy road that snakes down to **Sa Calobra** and the **Torrent de Pareis**. From the parking lot, follow the path through a cave and finally to the start of a river. In summer, this is a beach. In winter, expect to get wet. Follow the river by climbing the rocks alongside it. And take time to check out the ECHO. . .echo. . . cho. . .ooo. . .oo. . .in stereo!

Mallorca's east coast is just the opposite of the western mountains. It's flat, hot, and full of long, wide beaches. One of the best places to head to is **Porto Cristo**. Not because of its beaches and not because of its boat trips (although they're fun) but because of its huge **Cuevas del Drach**. These enormous "Dragon Caves" are an adventure to explore. Your imagination will be working overtime as you pass things like "the ruined castle" and "monster skulls." But you'll really be bowled over when you get to **Lake Martel**, one of the biggest underground lakes in the world. Sit in the front row and experience a rowboat concert

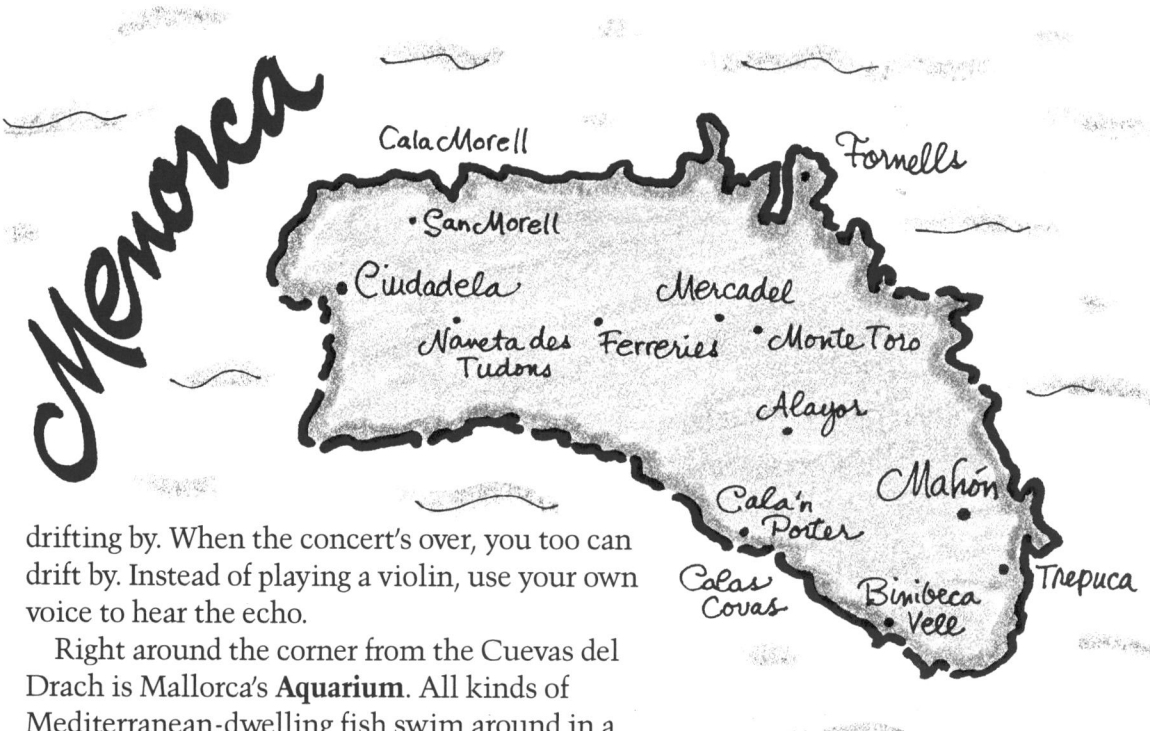

Menorca

Cala Morell
San Morell
Ciudadela
Naveta des Tudons
Ferreries
Mercadel
Monte Toro
Alayor
Mahón
Cala'n Porter
Colas Covas
Binibeca Vell
Trepuca
Fornells

drifting by. When the concert's over, you too can drift by. Instead of playing a violin, use your own voice to hear the echo.

Right around the corner from the Cuevas del Drach is Mallorca's **Aquarium**. All kinds of Mediterranean-dwelling fish swim around in a big tank here. See who you're swimming with in the ocean!

Menorca

Menorca is the second largest Balearic island. Look for prehistoric monuments wherever you go. These monuments are big mysteries: no one is quite sure who built them when, or even why. The first thing to do is to find a good map of the island. Ask for the archaeological map. Menorca has more beaches than all the other islands combined, and you'll need this map to find them.

Mahón (sometimes called Maó) is Menorca's capital city. British forces occupied Mahón from 1708 to 1802, so there's a lot of British influence here. This is a big plus, since most people speak English. But you should still try out your Catalán or Spanish; it's only polite.

Are you sick of beaches, resorts, and tourists? **_Picadero de Menorca_** _(the Menorcan School of Riding) will help you out. You can choose between a long, lazy ride around Antonio's_ finca _(farm) or all-day excursions around the islands. Either way you'll spend lots of time with a gentle horse, a friendly owner, and all the chickens, roosters, geese, turkeys, and cats you could ever wish for._

Mahón's steep streets are fun to get lost in. Try and work your way down to the harbor. As you walk, you'll see lots of yachts to your left and restaurants to your right. If you're hungry for more than the salty sea air, sink your teeth into the **Pizzeria Roma**. Going the other way, you'll hit the small **Aquarium**, which doubles as a bar. Snack right next to a moray eel—that should give you a chill. Next to the Aquarium is the **Xoiriguer Gin Factory**. You won't want to drink any of the offerings, but it's fun to see how the gin and herbal liqueurs are made.

During the Stone Age, many cave people made their oceanview homes at **Calas Covas**. If you'd like to see them, just take the cliff walk that starts from Cala'n Porter. You'll first walk by a big one that's been turned into a bar (the **Cova d'en Xoroi**) and then continue on to less crowded caves. Don't snoop too much; some of the caves are now inhabited by people seeking a simpler, Stone Age existence.

Do you like ice cream? Does a fish have lips?? **La Menorquina ice cream** from **Alayor** has a great reputation. Stop by their Alayor ice cream parlor and try it out. Alayor is also the cheese capital of Menorca. Predictably, you'll see lots of cows nearby.

Menorca's highest point is Monte Toro. As you make your way up (by foot or car) you'll get a fairy tale view of green rolling hills, cows (of course), and ocean. On a really clear day you can see as far as Mallorca, 35 miles away.

Ciudadela, on the opposite side of the island, is opposite in feel, too. While Mahón absorbed British culture, Ciudadela is more Moorish. Before the British landed, this was Menorca's capital. There's a sleepier feel here, and you'll notice the difference in buildings right away. Low, white arches replace British-style window apartments. Get a scoop of all-natural ice cream at **Baixomar**, by the cathedral, and then walk through the port to see some colorful fishing boats and town characters.

Ibiza

Of all the islands, Ibiza has the most fashionable reputation. This is the island where you'll find movie stars, fashion designers, and would-be's. One of the neatest things about Ibiza is its internationalism. People from all over the world have settled down on the island, and you'll hear different languages and accents wherever you go.

Ibiza Town is called "La Ciudad" by islanders. There are great beaches around, as well as cafés, boutiques, and restaurants. Sit by the harbor with a glass of fresh O.J. and watch the world go by. The **D'Alt Vila** (Old Town) is a shimmering old castle enclosed by high walls. You'll get some great views of the harbor from up here—and also run into the **Museo D'Alt Vila**, an archaeological museum that might teach you something about Ibiza's earliest beachgoers.

As with the other islands, you'll want to get hold of a good map. Ibiza's pretty **beaches** are hidden behind cliffs and woods and are sometimes hard to get to. For that reason, if you can find them, they're usually uncrowded. But remember to bring plenty of sunscreen, drinking water, and a picnic. Most of these quiet beaches don't have any facilities.

Santa Eulalia is a small town north of La Ciudad. Its square is usually full of craftspeople

selling their wares. Another fun spot is the **Es Cana Hippie Market**, where refugees from the 1960s sell handcrafted items. This is a good place to buy souvenirs as well as drift back twenty years in time.

On the other side of the island is **San Antonio**, Ibiza's only built-up resort. Take a walk around the harbor area and decide which **boat tour** you'd like to take. You can explore almost the entire island by boat, so if you have a desire to feel the sea breeze in your hair, this is the place to do it. A good nearby escape from the crowds is at **Punta Galera**, where you can swim off the sandy rocks that line the water.

A further escape by boat is to **Formentera**, the smallest inhabited island of the Balearics. For nearly 300 years, it was left uninhabited because of the Turkish pirates who roamed the area. The boat trip takes about an hour, and you may even see dolphins or flying fish on the way. On the island, you'll find empty beaches, friendly people, and even friendlier little green lizards that seem to pop up everywhere!

11. Adiós Muchachos y Muchachas

N ow that you've finished your trip to Spain, you probably feel much more worldly. And you are! You've probably learned some words in a new language. Maybe you have some things to remember Spain by—souvenirs, photos, drawings, or words—or maybe you feel like you'll remember it forever inside your head and heart. But you've brought something else back, too. You've learned how to get along with your global neighbors. So don't forget that old man who helped you onto the mule, or the kids you skateboarded with on the Ramblas. They're all the people next door.

¡Habla Español?

Spanish is spoken phonetically, just as it looks. Unlike English, there are hardly any exceptions to the rules.

You pronounce:

A like "Ah"	Soft C and Z like "Th"
E like "Eh?"	Soft G and J like "H"
I like "Ee"	Qu like "K"
O like "Oh"	R like you were rolling it
U like "Oo"	H is silent

Here are some words to help you get started. You might want to carry around a pocket dictionary. When you think of a word, look it up to see what it is in Spanish. And if someone is yelling, "Mira!" in your ear, you can look it up and see that it means "Look!"

Hello = Hola
Good-bye = Adiós, or Ciao (pronounced *chow*)
See ya later = Hasta luego
What's going on? = ¿Qué hay? (pronounced *kay eye*)
Nothing = Nada
How's it going? = ¿Qué tal?
Great = Muy bien
Badly = Mal
Do you speak English? = ¿Habla inglés?

¿Donde está el museo?

¡Lo siento!

ciao

¿Habla inglés?

Hasta luego

Soy Americana

¡Adiós!

Yes = Sí
No = No (this is an easy one!)
Please = Por favor
Thank you = Gracias
I'm sorry = Lo siento
Where is...? = ¿Donde está...?
   the museum = el museo
   the station = la estación
   the post office = el correo
   the town hall = el ayuntamiento
   this = este
Is it open? = ¿Está abierto?
Is it closed? = ¿Está cerrado?
Where are...? = ¿Donde están...?
   the bathrooms = los servicios
I (really) like = Me gusta (muchisimo)
I want... = Yo quiero...
How much does...cost? = ¿Cuánto cuesta...?
ice cream = helados
orange, apple, lemon, peach = naranja,
   manzana, limón, melecotón
orange juice = zumo de naranja
milk = leche
tea = té (another easy one)
hot chocolate = Colakao (regular) or chocolate
   (much thicker...yum!)
I am American (English) = Soy Americano/
   Americana (Inglés/Inglesa)

PRACTICE MAKES PERFECT

¡ Mil novecientos noventa y dos !

1992!

y tres! y cuatro! y . . .

1-10 = Uno, dos, tres, cuatro, cinco, seis, siete, ocho, nueve, diez
twenty = veinte
thirty = treinta
forty = cuarenta
fifty = cincuenta
sixty = sesenta
seventy = setenta
eighty = ochenta
ninety = noventa
one hundred = cien
two hundred = doscientos, three hundred = trescientos, etc.
five hundred = quinientos
one thousand = mil
two thousand = dos mil
1992 = mil novecientos noventa y dos
Monday = lunes
Tuesday = martes
Wednesday = miércoles
Thursday = jueves
Friday = viernes
Saturday = sábado
Sunday = domingo

Fiestas and Fun: What's Going On in Spain?

January
Epiphany: The Three Wise Men march and
 bring gifts
Tamborrada March in San Sebastian

February
Carnival (like Mardi Gras) in Cádiz and Sitges

March
Las Fallas in Valencia
Semana Santa in Sevilla, Toledo, and Cuenca

April
April Feria in Sevilla

May
Festival of Patios in Córdoba
Horse fair in Jerez de la Frontera
Fiesta de San Isidro in Madrid

June
Corpus Christi in Sevilla, Toledo, and Sitges
Dancing Egg, Barcelona Cathedral
International Festival of Music and Dance in
 Granada's Alhambra
Sunday *Curro* Roundups of Wild Horses in
 Galicia
Fiesta de San Juan (with horses) in Ciudadela,
 Menorca

July
Raiers Rafting Festival in Catalán Pyrenees
 (Llavorsi and around)
Basque Fiesta in Zumaya (near San Sebastian)
International Guitar Festival in Córdoba

Fiesta de San Fermín (Running of the Bulls) in
 Pamplona
Fiesta del Apóstol in Santiago de Compostela
San Sebastian International Jazz Festival
Open-Air Sculptures in Hecho (through
 August)
International Music Festival in Cadaques
Veranos de la Villa in Madrid
Greek Festival in Barcelona
The Moors and the Christians in Villajoyosa
 (near Alicante)

August
International Folklore Festival of the Pyrenees
 in Jaca (odd years)
Battle of the Christians and the Moors in
 Elche
International Fireworks Competition in San
 Sebastian
International Festival of Fantasy and Horror
 Films in Sitges
International Music and Ballet Festival in
 Santander
The Tomato Battle in Buñol (near Valencia)

September
18th-Century Bullfights in Ronda
La Virgen de la Merced in Barcelona

October
El Pilar Festival in Zaragoza
National Day (Columbus Day)

December
Christmas is especially good in Pamplona
New Year's Eve at Puerto del Sol, Madrid

Details

Hours and telephone numbers are not included. Hours are subject to change, and telephones can be hard to deal with since most people don't speak English. Most museums and sights are open Tuesday through Sunday (closed Mondays) from 9:00 a.m. to 1:00 p.m. and 5:00 to 8:00 p.m. To avoid disappointment, speak in English to anyone at Turismo, which is found in almost every Spanish town. This is also the best source for handicapped access information. Phone numbers are given with the area code first, in parentheses. You only have to dial the area code if you're outside the town's province. For information ahead of time, contact:

In the U.S.:
Spanish National Tourist Office
665 Fifth Avenue
New York, NY 10022
(212) 759-8822

In Canada:
Spanish National Tourist Office
102 Bloor Street West
14th Floor
Toronto, Ontario M5S 1M8
(416) 961-3131

In the U.K.:
Spanish National Tourist Office
57 St. James's Street
London SW1A 1LD
(01) 499-1169

Chapter 3. Taking the Bull by the Horns in Madrid

Alfredo's Barbacoa
Juan Hurtado de Mendoza, 11
Metro: Cuzco

California
Goya, 21
Metro: Velázquez

Casón del Buen Retiro
(home of Picasso's *Guernica*)
Alfonso XII, 88
Metro: Banco

Círculo de Bellas Artes and Café
Alcala, 42
Metro: Banco

Ciudad de Niños (Kid's City)
Casa de Campo Park
Metro: Lago

Edificio España café
Plaza de España
Metro: Plaza de España

El Corte Inglés
Preciados, 3
Metro: Sol

Estadio Santiago Bernabeu (Soccer Stadium)
Paseo de la Castellana, 142
Metro: Nuevos Ministerios

Foster's Hollywood
Princesa, 3 (and other locations)
Metro: Plaza de España

Las Ventas Bullring
Alcala, 237
Metro: Ventas

McDonald's (the fancy one)
Corner of Calle Montera and Gran Vía
Metro: Gran Vía

Museo Arqueológico
Serrano, 13
Metro: Colón

Museo de Artes Decorativas
Montalbán, 12
Metro: Banco

Museo de Carruajes
Campo de Moro Park, behind Royal Palace
Metro: Opera

Museo de Ciencias Naturales
José Abascal, 2
Metro: Nuevos Ministerios

Museo del Ejército
Mendez Nuñez, 1
Metro: Banco

Museo de Jamón
San Jerónimo, 6
Metro: Sol

Museo Naval
Paseo del Prado, 5
Metro: Banco

Palacio Real
Plaza de Oriente
Metro: Opera

Parque de Atracciónes
Casa de Campo Park
Metro: Batan

Planetario de Madrid
Parque de Tierno Galvan
Metro: Mendez Alvaro

Rastro flea market
Ribera de Curtidores and around
Metro: La Latina

Real Fábrica de Tapices (Royal Tapestry
  Factory)
Fuenterrabia, 2
Metro: Menéndez Pelayo

Teleférico Station to Casa de Campo
Parque del Oeste
Off Paseo de Rosales, near Calle Buen Suceso
Metro: Plaza de España

Templo de Debod (Egyptian temple)
Parque del Oeste
Metro: Plaza de España

Turismo #1
Plaza Mayor, 3
Tel. (91) 266 5477
Metro: Opera or Sol

Turismo #2
Princesa, 1
Torre de Madrid
Metro: Plaza de España
Tel. (91) 241 2325

Zoo de Madrid
Casa de Campo Park
Metro: Batan

**Chapter 4. Around Madrid: Spanish Castle
Magic**

Aranjuez
Casa del Labrador
Jardín del Principe

Casa Marina
Jardín del Principe

Turismo
Plaza de Santiago Rusiñol
Tel. (91) 891 0427

Ávila
Convento de Santa Teresa
Plaza de la Santa

Museo Provincial
Casa de los Deanes
Plaza de Nalvillos, 3

Turismo
Plaza Catedral, 4
Tel. (918) 21 13 87

Cuenca
Museo de Arte Abstracto Español
Casas Colgadas
Calle Obispo
Near Plaza Mayor

Monasterio de Piedra
Follow signs from Calatayud (Aragón)

Salamanca
Old and New Cathedrals
Plaza de Anaya

Turismo #1
Gran Vía (España), 39-41
Tel. (923) 26 85 71

Turismo #2 (much smaller)
Plaza Mayor, 10
Tel. (923) 21 83 42

University of Salamanca
Patio de las Escuelas

Segovia
Alcázar
Plaza del Alcázar
End of Calle de los Leones

Cathedral
Plaza Mayor

Iglesia de la Vera Cruz
Carretera a Zamarramala

Roman aqueduct
Plaza de Azoguejo

Turismo
Plaza Mayor, 10
Tel. (911) 43 03 28

Toledo
Alcázar
Behind Plaza de Zocodover

Casa del Greco
Calle de los Amarillos

Cathedral
Entrance off Plaza Ayuntamiento

San Juan de los Reyes Monastery
Calle Reyes Católicos

Santo Tomé Church
El Greco's *The Burial of the Counts of Orgaz*
Travesio de Santo Tomé

Sephardic Museum (Jewish History)
Sinagoga del Tránsito
Calle Reyes Católicos

Turismo
Across from Puerta de Bisagra
Tel. (925) 22 08 43

**Chapter 5. Northern Spain:
Bagpipes and Beaches, Basques and Bikes**

Caberceno (Cantabria)
Natural Park and Zoo
Turnoff by Obregón, near Saron
17 km southeast of Santander

Cabo de Fisterra (Galicia)
C-543 to C-550, from Santiago

Comillas (Cantabria)
El Capricho
Follow signs

Cuevas de Puente Viesgo (Cantabria)
Carretera N-623, 28 km south of Santander
   (toward Logroño)
Cantabria

Nuria (The Pyrenees)
La Cremellera train
Ribes de Freser train station
Catalunya

Ordesa National Park (The Pyrenees)
C-140, 8 km past Torla
Aragón

Picos de Europa (Cantabria)
Teleférico de Fuente Dé
End of Route N-621

San Sebastian (Basque Country)
Aquarium
Paseo Nuevo, past the docks

Museo San Telmo
Plaza Ignacio Zuloaga

Pukas Surf Shop
corner of Kale Nagusia and Fermin
    Calbeton Kalea

Turismo
Victoria Eugenio Theater
Reina Regente, by 3rd bridge
Tel. (943) 42 10 02

Santander (Cantabria)
Mesón del Toroso
end of Calle Cuesta

Museo Maritimo del Cantabrico
San Martin de Bajamar, s/n

Museo de Prehistoria
Casimiro Sainz, 4

Palacio Real
Peninsula de la Magdalena

Turismo
Plaza Porticada, 1
Tel. (942) 31 07 08 or 31 07 56

Zoo de Santander
Peninsula de la Magdalena

Santiago de Compostela (Galicia)
Cathedral de Santiago
Praza Obradoira

Turismo
Rúa del Villar, 43
Tel. (981) 58 40 81

Santillana del Mar (Cantabria)
La Cueva de Altamira and Museo Prehistorica
2 km outside town

Turismo
Plaza Mayor
Tel. (942) 81 82 51

Zoo Santillana del Mar
on the edge of town

Vall D'Aran (The Pyrenees)
Musèu dera Val D'Aran
Carrèr Major, 26
Vielha

Baqueira/Beret ski resort
Off Route C-142, 19 km from Vielha

Chapter 6. ¡Barcelona Mès Que Mai!

2 Bis Gift Shop
Calle Bisbe, 2
Metro: Jaume I

Casa Battló
Passeig de Gràcia, 43
Metro: Passeig de Gràcia

Casa Milá (La Pedrera)
Passeig de Gràcia, 92
Metro: Diagonal

Cathedral
Plaça de la Seu
Metro: Jaume I

Chocolateria Dulcinea
Carrer de Petritxol, off Plaça del Pi
Metro: Liceu

El Corte Inglés
Plaça Catalunya, 14
Metro: Catalunya

El Ingenio
Calle Rauric
Metro: Liceu

El Laberint d'Horta
Park behind Velodrome
Bus #27 from Plaça Catalunya

Estadi Camp Nou (Soccer Stadium)
Off Avenida Aristides Maillol
Metro: Collblanc

Fonts Luminoses
Palau Nacional
Montjuïc Park
Metro: Espanya

Fundació Joan Miró
Plaça Neptú
Montjuïc Park
Metro: Espanya

Gran Teatro del Liceu
Ramblas, 61
(corner of Sant Pau)
Metro: Liceu

Holoscope-Holography Museum
Calle St. Jaume I, 1
Metro: Jaume I
May be closed in August

Hospital de Santa Creu
Calle Hospital, 56
(2 blocks from Ramblas)
Metro: Liceu

Mercat Sant Josep (La Boqueria)
Plaça de la Boqueria, on the Ramblas
Metro: Liceu

Mies van der Rohe Pavilion
Montjuïc Park
Metro: Espanya

Monument a Colom
Plaça Portal de la Pau
(End of the Ramblas facing the sea)
Metro: Drassanes

Museu Arqueològic
Montjuïc Park
Metro: Espanya

Museu d'Art de Catalunya
Palau Nacional
Montjuïc Park
Metro: Espanya

Museu de Calzados (Shoe Museum)
Plaça Sant Felip Neri
Metro: Jaume I

Museu de Cera (Wax Museum)
Pasaje de la Banca, 7
Metro: Drassanes

Museu de Ciencia
Teodoro Roviralta, 55
Ferrocarriles Catalanes train from
Pl. Catalunya to Avda. Tibidabo

Museu Etnològic
Passeig Santa Madrona
Montjuïc Park
Metro: Espanya

Museu de Historia Natural
Plaça Real
Metro: Liceu

Museu Maritim (*Drassanes*)
Reales Atarazanes, at end of Ramblas
Metro: Drassanes

Museu Militar
in Castell de Barcelona
Montjuïc Park
Teleférico from Avinguda de l'Estadi

Museu Picasso
Calle Montcada, 15
Metro: Jaume I

Palau de Virreina
(What's going on?)
Rambla, 99
Metro: Liceu

Palau Real-Royal Palace
Plaça del Rei
Metro: Jaume I

Parc d'Atraccions
Montjuïc Park
Teleférico from Avinguda de l'Estadi
or Metro: Paral-lel

Parc d'Atraccions
Monte Tibidabo
Ferrocarriles Catalanes train from
Pl. Catalunya to Avda. Tibidabo,
then funicular train to top

Poble Espanyol
Montjuïc Park
Metro: Espanya

Sagrada Família
Between Mallorca-Provença and Marina-
  Sardenya streets
Metro: Sagrada Família

Turismo #1
Gran Vía, 658 (corner of Pau Claris)
Metro: Catalunya or Urquinaona
Tel. (93) 301 7443 or 317 2246

Turismo #2
In Ajuntament (city hall)
Plaça de Sant Jaume
Metro: Jaume I
Tel. (93) 318 2525

Zoo de Barcelona
Parc de la Ciutadella
Metro: Arc de Triomf

Chapter 7. Costa Catalunya

Cadaques
Museu Perrot-Moore
Plaça Federico Rahola

Turismo
Cotche 2A
Tel. (972) 25 83 15

Calella
Jardines de Cap Roig
Follow signs

Delta de l'Ebre Natural Park
Ecomuseu and Centro de Información
Plaça del 20 de Maig
Deltebre

Figueres
Museu Dalí
Plaça Gala-Dalí

Museu de Joguets
Rambla, 10

Turismo
Plaça del Sol
in front of post office building
Tel. (972) 50 31 55

Girona
Banys Arabs (Arab Baths)
Behind cathedral

Caterra restaurant
Calle Ballesteries

Cathedral
End of Calle de la Força

Centre Isaac El Cec
Up the stairs from Calle de la Força

Museu Arqueològic
Santa Lucía, 1 (across bridge)

Turismo
Plaça del Vi, 1
Tel. (972) 20 26 79

Monestir de Sant Pere de Rodes
Off Llanca-Selva road, follow signs

Tarragona
Café Mel i Mata
Carrer Major (near Pl. del Font)

Museu Arqueològic
Plaça del Rei

Museu Historic
next to Museu Arqueològic

La Puda restaurant
El Sollér

Necropolis
Avinguda Ramon y Cajal

Puente del Diablo (Devil's Bridge Aqueduct)
4 km toward A-7 freeway out of town

Turismo #1
Rambla Nova, 46
Tel. (972) 23 21 43

Turismo #2
Carrer Major, 39
Below cathedral steps
Tel. (972) 23 89 22

Toroella de Montgri
Castell del Misteri Magic Show
Carrer Esglesia, 10
Tel. (972) 76 09 00

Tossa de Mar
Dino's Pizzeria
Calle San Telmo, 28

Museu Municipal
Vila Vella

Vila Romana
Corner Carrer Miramar and Avinguda Costa
  Brava

Turismo
At bus station
Carretera de Lloret
Tel. (972) 34 01 08

Chapter 8. A Wind from the East

Alicante
Boats to Tabarca Island
Near end of Explanade de España

Castello de Santa Barbara
Elevator stop opposite Playa Postiguet

Museo de Arte de Siglo XX
Plaza de Santa Maria, 3

Turismo
Explanade de España, 2
Tel. (96) 521 2285

Aqualandia
North of Benidorm off N-332

Calpe
Turismo
Avenida Ejércitos Españoles, 66
Tel. (96) 583 1250

Coves de Canalobre
Follow signs from Busot
(off N-332 or N-340)

Denia
Museu Arqueològic
At the top of the castle

Turismo
Patricio Ferrandiz
Near Pl. de Jorge Juan
Tel. (96) 578 0957

Elche
Huerta del Cura
Calle Federico García Sanchíz

Turismo
Parque Municipal
Tel. (96) 545 2747

Gandía
Turismo
Marqués de Campo
Across from train station
Tel. (96) 287 4544

Grutas de Sant Josep
Follow signs from Vall de Uixó
Off N-340,
About 40 km north of Valencia

Jijona
Turrón El Lobo
Follow signs

Valencia
Cathedral and Miguelete
Plaza de la Virgen

Centro de Arte Moderno Julio Gonzalez
Guillem de Castro, 118

Horchatería El Siglo
Plaza Santa Catalina

Horchatería Santa Catalina
Plaza Santa Catalina

Jardì Botànic
Calle Beato Gaspar Bono

La Lonja (Silk Exchange)
Plaza del Mercado

Libreria Inglesa
Calle Conde Trenor, 4

Mercado Central
Plaza del Mercado

Museo de Bellas Artes
San Pio V, 9
(in Jardines del Real)

Museo de Fallas
Plaza Monte Olivete, 4

Museu Historic
Inside Ayuntamiento (town hall)
Plaza de Ayuntamiento, 1

Museo Nacional de Cerámica
Palacio del Marques de Dos Aguas
Poeta Querol, 2

Museo Taurino
Pasaje Doctor Serra, next to the bullring

Palau de Musica
Avenida Jacinto

Turismo #1
Paz, 48
Tel. (96) 352 4000

Turismo #2
Plaza del Ayuntamiento, 1
Tel. (96) 351 0417

Tourist Hotline
Tel. (96) 352 4000

Chapter 9. The South: Moors, Mountains, and More

Antequera
Cueva de Menga
2 km outside town on road to Málaga

Turismo
Palacio de Nájera
Coso Viejo
Tel. (952) 84 14 27

AquaPark
MA-408 outside Torremolinos

Córdoba
Museo Taurino (Bullfight Museum)
Plaza Maimonides

Sinagoga
Calle Judio

Torre de Calahorra
Living Museum of Andalucía
Opposite Mezquita over Puente Romano

Turismo
Torrijos, 10
Next to La Mezquita mosque
Tel. (957) 47 12 35

Turismo #2
Plaza de Judás Levi
Tel. (957) 29 07 40

Zoco Crafts Market
Behind Museo Taurino

Coto Doñana National Park
Centro de Recepción de Acebuche
Off Route H-312, 4 km from Matalascañas
Reservations: (955) 24 50 92
They speak English

Cueva de la Pileta
On MA-501, about 28 km from Ronda

El Torcal National Park
Off Route C-3310
12 km south of Antequera

Gibraltar
Gibraltar Museum
Bomb House Lane

Top of the Rock Cable Car Station
End of Main Street

Tourist Office
Cathedral Square

Granada
The Alhambra
Up Cuesta de Gomerez

Capilla Real
Calle de Reyes

Sacramonte Caves
Past the Cuesta de Chapiz

Turismo #1
Libreros, 2
Tel. (958) 22 66 88

Turismo #2
Inside Patronato
Pl. Mariana Pineda, 10
Tel. (958) 22 66 88

Italica Roman ruins
In Santiponce, 9 km from Sevilla

Jerez de la Frontera
Andalusian Riding School
Call ahead of time, they speak English
Tel. (956) 31 11 11

Turismo
Alameda Cristina, 7
Tel. (956) 33 11 50

Las Alpujarras
Global Turismo
Carretera de la Sierra
Bubión
Tel. (958) 76 32 36

Málaga
Alcazaba and Gibralfaro Castle
At end of Paseo del Parque

Turismo
Marqués de Larios, 5
Tel. (952) 21 34 45

Marbella
Turismo
Miguel Cano, 1
Tel. (952) 77 14 42

Mijas
Carramoto de Max
Miniatures Museum
Plaza Principal

Burro Taxis
Plaza Principal

Ronda
Plaza de Toros (Bullring)
Calle Virgen de la Paz

Turismo
Plaza de España, 1
Tel. (952) 87 12 72

Sevilla
Alcázar
Entrance in Plaza del Triunfo

Cathedral and Giralda
Plaza Virgen de los Reyes

Los Gallos *flamenco* show
Plaza Santa Cruz

La Maestranza Bullring
Plaza de Toros
Off Paseo de Colon

Torre de Oro
(and Naval Museum)
Paseo de Colon, near San Telmo bridge

Turismo
Avenida de la Constitución, 21
Tel. (954) 22 14 04

Solynieve Ski Area
On route GR-420 to Veleta

Tivoli World
MA-408 between Torremolinos and Mijas

Yucca City/Mini Hollywood
Intersection of N-340 and C-3326
About 25 km north of Almeria

Chapter 10. A Slice of Island Life

Ibiza
Boat to Formentera
La Ciudad Harbor

Museo D'Alt Vila
Plaza de la Catedral
Ibiza Town (La Ciudad)

Turismo
Vara del Rey, 13
Ibiza Town
Tel. (971) 30 19 00

Mallorca
Bellver Castle
El Arenal

Sa Granja (Folk Museum)
Near Banyulbafar

Train to Soller
Plaza España
Palma

Turismo
Avenida Jaime III, 10
Palma
Tel. (971) 71 22 16

Turismo
Plaza de España
Palma

Menorca
Aquarium/Bar
Anden de Poniente, waterfront

La Menorquina Ice Cream Parlor
Carrer Nou
Alayor

Picadero de Menorca-Horse riding
Señor Antonio Marques
Follow signs on Alayor-Mercadel road
He speaks English
Tel. (971) 37 18 52

Pizzeria Roma
Anden de Levante, 295
Mahón

Turismo
Plaza Explanada, 40
Mahón
Tel. (971) 36 37 90

Xoiriguer Gin Factory
Anden de Poniente, waterfront
Mahón

Kidding Around with John Muir Publications

We are making the world more accessible for young travelers. In your hand you have one of several John Muir Publications guides written and designed especially for kids. We will be *Kidding Around* other cities also. Send us your thoughts, corrections, and suggestions. We also publish other young readers titles as well as adult books about travel and other subjects. Let us know if you would like one of our catalogs. All the titles below are 64 pages and $9.95, except for *Kidding Around the National Parks of the Southwest* and *Kidding Around Spain*, which are 108 pages and $12.95 each.

TITLES NOW AVAILABLE IN THE SERIES
Kidding Around Atlanta
Kidding Around Boston
Kidding Around Chicago
Kidding Around the Hawaiian Islands
Kidding Around London
Kidding Around Los Angeles
Kidding Around the National Parks of the Southwest
Kidding Around New York City
Kidding Around Paris
Kidding Around Philadelphia
Kidding Around San Diego
Kidding Around San Francisco
Kidding Around Santa Fe
Kidding Around Seattle
Kidding Around Spain
Kidding Around Washington, D.C.

Ordering Information
Your books will be sent to you via UPS (for U.S. destinations). UPS will not deliver to a P.O. Box; please give us a street address. Include $2.75 for the first item ordered and $.50 for each additional item to cover shipping and handling costs. For airmail within the U.S., enclose $4.00. All foreign orders will be shipped surface rate; please enclose $3.00 for the first item and $1.00 for each additional item. Please inquire about foreign airmail rates.

Method of Payment
Your order may be paid by check, money order, or credit card. We cannot be responsible for cash sent through the mail. All payments must be made in U.S. dollars drawn on a U.S. bank. Canadian postal money orders in U.S. dollars are acceptable. For VISA, MasterCard, or American Express orders, include your card number, expiration date, and your signature, or call (800) 888-7504. Books ordered on American Express cards can be shipped only to the billing address of the cardholder. Sorry, no C.O.D.'s. Residents of sunny New Mexico, add 5.875% tax to the total.

Address all orders and inquiries to:
John Muir Publications
P.O. Box 613
Santa Fe, NM 87504
(505) 982-4078
(800) 888-7504